The Illustrated Encyclopedia of the *Animal Kingdom*

The Danbury Press

Editorial direction and supervision for the English language edition by PERCY KNAUTH.

Associate Editor—DALE MCADOO.

Art direction and design by JACK JAGET.

Volume 2—Adapted by BARBARA MILLER.

Zoological Advisory Board

JOSEPH A. DAVIS, Curator of Mammals, New York Zoological Society
ROBERT S. DE SANTO, Assistant Professor of Zoology, Connecticut College, New London, Conn.
PATRICIA DUDLEY, Department of Biological Sciences, Barnard College,
    Columbia University, New York, N.Y.
ROBERT E. SMOLKER, Associate Professor of Biology, State University of New York, Stonybrook, N.Y.
RICHARD G. VAN GELDER, Chairman & Curator, Department of Mammalogy, The
    American Museum of Natural History, New York, N.Y.
RICHARD G. ZWEIFEL, Chairman & Curator, Department of Herpetology, The American
    Museum of Natural History, New York, N.Y.

The Danbury Press, a division of Grolier Enterprises, Inc.
    Publisher—ROBERT B. CLARKE.
    Marketing Director—ROBERT G. BARTNER.
    Creative Director—GILBERT EVANS.
    Publishing Consultant—DAVID MENDELSOHN.
    Assistant to the Publisher—VALERIE HARBOUR.

PHOTO CREDITS

Volume II

Sig. Anderloni—Cormano, 103; Barnaby's Picture Library—42, 65; Cremella di Barzano, 122; Baschiere—Salvadori, 37; Blossom
Natural History Photographic Agency—Betsoms, 127; Carlo Dani, 92, 94, 95, 97, 98, 100, 101, 111; E. Dulevant—Torino, 114;
M. Fantin, 82; Lucio Gaggero, 119; Ingmar Holmasen, Malmkoping, 47, 118, 139; Institut Pour La Recherche Scientifique
Centrale-Lwiro, 40, 41, 47, 142, 143; London Zoological Society, 50, 51, 65, 68; Marchetti—Viareggio, 115; Margiocco—8, 9, 18, 26,
30, 49, 57, 66, 75, 76, 77, 125, Meston Specialties—59; Olimpic Natural History Association—24; Charlie Ott—67; Circo di Moira
Orfei—85; Willis Peterson, 22, 112, 135; Paul Popper—London, 36, 43, 48, 52, 53, 69, 70, 71, 84, 85, 120, 124, 131; Roebild—71,
Emu—17, Muller—34, McCutcheon, 143; A. P. Rossi—27; H. H. Schroder—138, 141, S.C.M. General Biological Inc.—Chicago—121;
Sirman-Dimt—74; Tomsich—56, 62, 96; World Wildlife Fund-Morges—66, 70; Allo Zoo di Colonia—68; Esquita Allo Zoo di
Francoforte Sul Meno—46, 72; Zoo di Minano-Gelmetti—73; M. Wiedman—6, 7, 28, 29, 58, 86, 88.

CONTENTS

With this second volume, the emphasis of the series shifts from the broad picture of animal life presented in Volume I to an informative, detailed and comprehensive coverage of each of the various animal groups, taken in scientific sequence. Starting with the meat-eating mammals, successive volumes deal with birds, reptiles, fish, insects and many others.

The Carnivores

Introducing the Meat-eaters

An amoeba absorbing another one-celled animal can be called a carnivore, or meat-eater, along with the lion, wolf and weasel. From the very beginning of life some animals have always eaten others, and in a sense all those which feed on the flesh and bones of other animals can be called meat-eaters.

During the course of their 500 million years of evolution, vertebrates (the animals with backbones) have blossomed out into a great variety of carnivores. The first vertebrates were jawless fishes; they sucked up mud and filtered out their food at the bottom of bodies of fresh water. When the first amphibians, the first vertebrates to adapt to the land, crawled out of the water, they fed on spiders and scorpions. But it wasn't until the reptiles took over the earth, about 215 million

A pride of lions basks in the sun on the African plain. These animals, after a heavy meal, may not need to eat again for a week, since they consume prodigious amounts of meat at a single kill.

years ago, that the vertebrates divided into flesh-eaters (carnivores) and plant-eaters (herbivores).

That different kinds of reptiles preferred different kinds of food is shown by the study of fossils, which are the remains or impressions in rock of ancient animals or plants. Such studies reveal differences in the structure of the body, especially in the structure of the jaws and teeth. Plant-eaters are generally bulky, since they have to take in and process a great quantity of plants in order to obtain the nourishment they need. Carnivores with their protein-rich diet require less food. Herbivores have teeth adapted for grinding and chopping green plants, whereas the carnivores' teeth are suited for stabbing, slicing and tearing.

During the Age of Reptiles, when dinosaurs dominated the land (between 135 and 181 million years ago), the lines were already drawn between herbivores and carnivores. Giant flesh-eaters such as the 35-foot-long, two-footed *Allosaurus* preyed on impressive plant-eaters such as the 70-foot-long, four-footed *Brontosaurus* and the many other varieties with ducklike bills or curious knobs and spines on their skulls. Mammals—animals whose young suckle milk from the mammary or milk glands of the mother—already existed in those reptilian days but they played a relatively unimportant role. It was

Beautifully coordinated body movements made possible by a powerful musculature and a highly developed intelligence due to the large size of the brain, as shown in the skull below, combine to make this leopard a fine example of a highly advanced carnivore.

not until that still mysterious event, the extinction of the great dinosaurs, that mammals evolved into the many kinds of carnivores and herbivores known today. This evolution began with small insect-eaters, some of which needed only to increase in size and modify their teeth to become carnivores. Consequently, as vegetation-eating mammals evolved, there also evolved a group of flesh-eating mammals to prey on them, and herbivorous and carnivorous mammals rapidly filled the vacuum left by the now extinct dinosaurs. These first carnivorous mammals are called creodonts. Slow-moving and rather stupid, they preyed on herbivores called condylarths. From then on, there was a constant

nated movements; and of the senses smell, vision and hearing, one or more are keen. They live on the ground, in the trees or in the water. They range from the tiny weasels to the great grizzly bears, from the playful raccoon to the lion and back to our friend the tabby cat, and from the river otters to the sea lions. They also include the unjustly despised hyena and the much loved dog.

What Are the Carnivores?

The animals technically called carnivores can best be defined in terms of certain anatomical characteristics. They generally have lithe, powerful bodies. They have powerful

The thylacine, sometimes called a Tasmanian "wolf" (near left), is a mammal that feeds on meat. It does not belong to the order of the carnivores, however, but to that of the marsupials. Its skull (below) cannot be confused with that of a true carnivore. The cat (far left) is a true carnivore. In contrast to the thylacine, which has eight upper incisors, the cat has six.

evolutionary give-and-take between the meat-eaters and the animals upon which they preyed. As herbivores learned to run faster and think more quickly, so did carnivores, in order to catch them. The brains, brawn and teeth of carnivores became increasingly better suited for success in hunting. Some even took to the water and adopted a completely aquatic life.

Today's carnivores include some of the most alert and intelligent of mammals. They have well developed brains, quick, coordi-

jaws and four or five toes on each foot equipped with sharp claws. They are all mammals and mostly carnivorous, but some also eat plants. But to complicate the definition, it must also be said that the carnivorous way of life is shared by many different animals which are not mammals and not even vertebrates. Carrion beetles finish the meat left by hyenas: are both not equally carnivorous? Hawks and eagles are great hunters, and even chickens pick at meat. All this demonstrates that a shared preference for a cer-

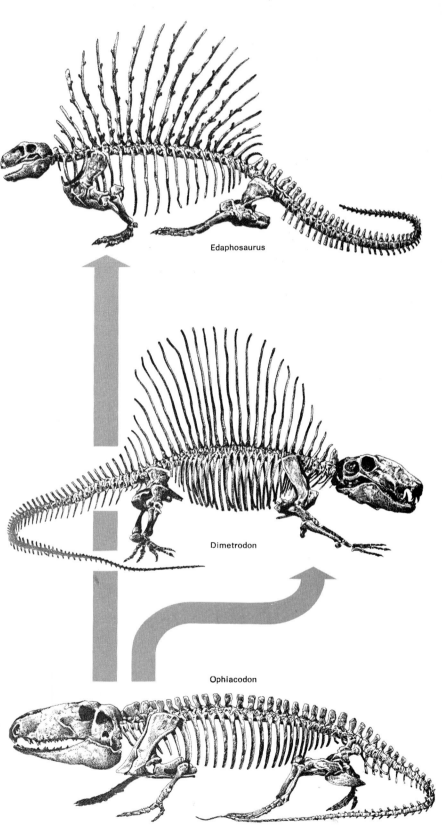

Edaphosaurus

Dimetrodon

Ophiacodon

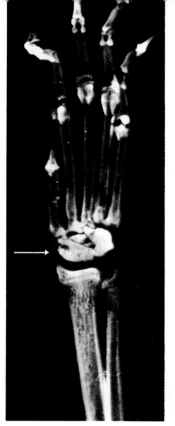
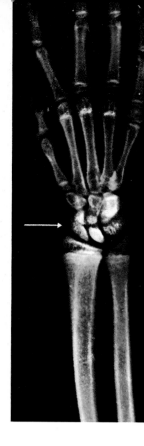

tain *kind* of food does not necessarily indicate a close relationship. It is only by tracing evolutionary lineages that we can arrive at a good definition of what constitutes a related group of animals. Among the placental mammals, for instance (those whose young grow within the mother's body), there are a number of subgroups whose teeth and body features distinguish them from one another—hallmarks not shared by any other "order," as the subgroup is called. Carnivores are such an order; rodents (rats, mice etc.) are another.

These hallmarks are the result of the ability of animals to adapt to the demands of their world. Carnivorous animals always evolve where the environment provides sufficient game on which they can prey for food. Starting with such a basic formula, the order of carnivora can be further defined by breaking it down into "families," again distinguishable by anatomical peculiarities. These "fam-

ilies" are the weasels, the dogs, the hyenas, the bears, the raccoons, the civets, the cats, the hair seals, the fur seals and the walruses. But because carnivorous animals develop where there is sufficient food, they have also evolved on the marsupial side of mammalian stock, among the animals which carry their young in external pouches. Such was the case in Australia. Opossumlike marsupials invaded this continent while it was still connected to Asia. Then, about 70 million years ago, Australia was isolated before placental mammals had been able to enter. Thus marsupials reigned uncontested and evolved into many different types. One group became carnivorous, and to this day Australia harbors catlike marsupials, the wolflike Tasmanian wolf and the wolverinelike Tasmanian devil. Another proof that carnivores evolve where there is sufficient game is the plight of marsupials in South America. Originally they migrated south over a land bridge, the Isthmus of Pan-

ama, which was subsequently inundated. Marsupials flourished on the southern continent because they were unchallenged, and they developed such carnivorous forms as sabre-toothed cats and other animals as big as bears. Then the bridge was reestablished and the continent was invaded by placental dogs and cats coming from North America and vanquishing the carnivorous marsupials.

The order of placental carnivores is set apart from all other mammals by a number of characteristics common only to it. One of its most important features is the arrangement of teeth. The eyeteeth, or canines, are lengthened into sharp fangs. Along the sides of the jaw, one upper and one lower tooth (the last upper premolar and the first lower molar) are shaped like blades, making them very effective shearing tools. These are the *carnassials*.

Carnivores also have a particular system for opening their jaws. The lower jaw is at-

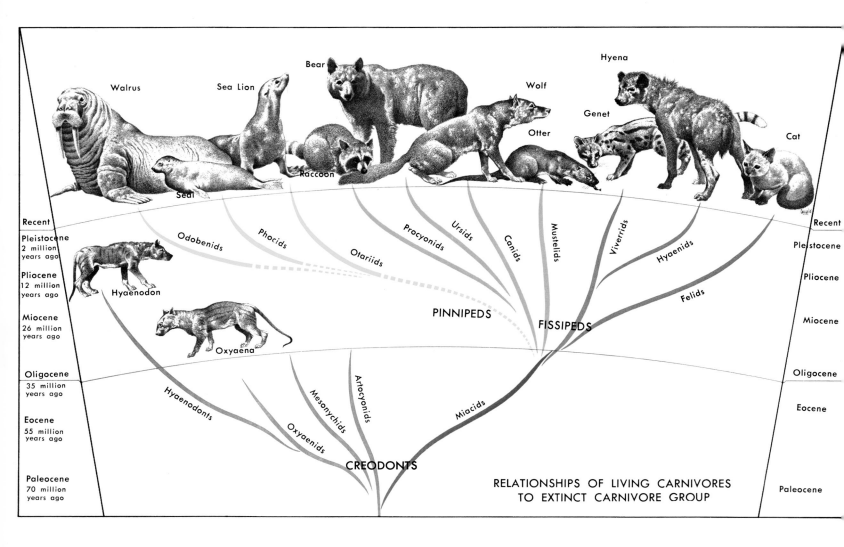

Recent	Recent
Pleistocene 2 million years ago	Pleistocene
Pliocene 12 million years ago	Pliocene
Miocene 26 million years ago	Miocene
Oligocene 35 million years ago	Oligocene
Eocene 55 million years ago	Eocene
Paleocene 70 million years ago	Paleocene

Walrus · Sea Lion · Bear · Hyena · Wolf · Genet · Otter · Cat · Raccoon · Seal

Odobenids · Phocids · Otariids · Procyonids · Ursids · Canids · Mustelids · Viverrids · Hyaenids · Felids

PINNIPEDS · FISSIPEDS

Hyaenodon · Oxyaena

Hyaenodonts · Oxyaenids · Mesonychids · Arctocyonids · Miacids

CREODONTS

RELATIONSHIPS OF LIVING CARNIVORES
TO EXTINCT CARNIVORE GROUP

Modern carnivore families evolved from a single stock, called the miacids, some 35 million years ago. Before that there were several groups of archaic carnivores called creodonts, all of which are now extinct.

The modern carnivores fall into two groups: the land carnivores, or fissipeds, and the marine carnivores, or pinnipeds.

tached in such a way that a side-to-side movement is difficult but a large gape, or top to bottom opening, is possible. This is all in key with the stabbing and slicing of meat and quite different from the jaws of herbivores, where side-to-side movements of the jaws help in grinding up plant food.

Although some carnivores walk on their toes and others on their soles, both kinds share the fusion of certain bones in the wrist, making this joint capable of moving only up and down and not sideways. This anatomical construction ties in with the general

lack of a collar bone, another feature related to a mainly forward-and-backward movement of the front limbs. Animals that use sideways movements of the hands and limbs while climbing, such as monkeys, all have unfused wristbones and well developed collar bones.

The carnivore brain is distinguished by its relatively large size and the considerable development of its higher centers. These are neurological features related to the high degree of alertness and intelligence necessary for the hunting of fast-moving game.

Carnivores of the Past

Having listed the main characteristics (or *characters*, as zoologists say) of the order Carnivora as it exists today, we shall now examine how these various adaptations that turned certain mammals into efficient hunters of moving prey came about.

As we have seen, the basic stock of placental mammals from which all the modern orders are derived had lived very much in the shadow of the dominant reptiles until most of these became extinct some 70 million years ago. After this, the survivors, the insectivores, which include shrews, moles and hedgehogs among their modern representatives, were then able to diversify into the many kinds of mammals, all archaic forms that filled the ecological roles left vacant by the reptiles. Among these were the creodonts, the primitive flesh-eaters, and the condylarths, which include most of the first herbivores.

The creodonts and the condylarths are actually quite closely related, and it appears from the fossil evidence that an early, mainly flesh-eating stock, derived from an insectivore ancestry, gave rise to both these kinds of archaic mammals. In particular, the even-toed hoofed mammals (e.g. pigs, deer, sheep, cattle) seem to be very closely related to some of the early creodonts. The odd-toed hoofed mammals (horses, tapirs and rhinos) form an entirely separate assemblage descended from the condylarths, and, strange as it may seem, a cow, for example, is as closely related to a lion as to a horse.

The development of carnivores was a logical consequence of the evolving habits of the ancestral insectivores. Once large plant-eating forms had come into being, it was only to be expected that other forms should prey upon them and acquire various tools to fit them for a flesh-eating existence.

A good set of front teeth (the incisors) for biting off flesh and a pair of piercing eye-teeth (canines) were already present in the insectivores and required little modification, other than additional emphasis on the canines. The cheek teeth, however, were the ones that came in for a lot of change. For purposes of eating flesh, some sort of shearing apparatus to slice off the meat and cut through sinews is a necessity. While the insectivores have some shearing action between the back edge of each upper cheek tooth and

This skull (above) belonged to Smilodon, *a saber-tooth "tiger." The sabers show distinctly in the picture, as does the enormous opening of which the jaw was capable. Mastodons were the chief prey of this carnivore, which would swing the jaw wide and strike like a snake with the long fangs.*

Oxyaena, *pictured at the left, was a creodont that flourished some 60 million years ago. In its tooth structure, the first upper and the second lower molar were carnassials.*

the front edge of the following lower one, the carnivores developed a highly efficient shear between a pair of very specialized cheek teeth—the carnassials. These teeth became simplified in structure, growing high, narrow and elongated.

In the early carnivores, the creodonts, the particular pair of cheek teeth that developed into carnassials varied. It was as though natural selection was "experimenting." In the modern carnivores and their direct ancestors, it is always the last premolar above and the first molar below that form the carnassial set, but in some creodonts the pair developed was

very long, but neither were the toes much reduced in length except for the first digit (like our thumb), which gradually became useless and finally disappeared. We can imagine the earliest carnivores as small, probably tree-climbing animals much like opossums in their general habits. They walked, like bears, on five-toed feet planted flat on the ground. Body and limbs were flexible, the skull long, the brain small.

From this beginning, the carnivores evolved in three stages. First, the creodonts evolved from the early insect-eaters. Second, an early family of creodonts branched out

Tritemnodon (right) was a creodont living approximately 50 million years ago. In its tooth structure, as in that of all the members of the family Hyaenodontidae, the second upper molar and the third lower molar were the carnassials.

The brain of the creodont (below), was almost totally without convolutions. This primitive condition does not exist in modern fissipeds, who have well-developed brains.

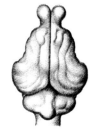

between cheek teeth further back in the jaw. Some ancient forms never developed carnassials at all, and other modern carnivores lost the ability to use them when they no longer needed them to chew food. The teeth behind the carnassials in animals eating only meat are smaller or nonexistent. Among others, such as the bears, with their diversified tastes, these teeth have become low-crowned crushing teeth, good for eating berries, fruits and nuts as well.

Because a carnivore uses its claws for seizing prey, there was never a need to develop hooves. Hand and foot bones never grew

into the modern land carnivores or fissipeds, animals whose feet had separated toes and were adapted for walking. Lastly, we have the pinnipeds, whose feet were webbed as an adaptation for life in the water.

The Creodonts were the earliest carnivores. Adapting and evolving successfully in their environment, they were the principal flesh-eating animals of the northern continents during the Paleocene and the Eocene, a time extending from 40 million to almost 60 million years ago. But as the early hoofed herbivores which served as prey began to disappear, the creodonts were replaced by more advanced carnivores, the fissipeds.

The oldest creodont family, the arctocyonids, was probably related to the primitive insectivores. Its members included both small and large forms. Two large kinds were the European *Arctocyon* and the American *Claenodon*, both as big as bears, with flattened claws and wolflike proportions. The largest known carnivore, then as now, was the giant *Andrewsarchus*, found in the late Eocene rocks of Mongolia, with a skull measuring

a wolf and from 2 to 4 feet long.

The Miacids, however, turned out to be the dominant family of the post-Eocene period. Small, forest-dwelling hunters about the size of weasels, they had long bodies and tails and flexible limbs. They had carnassial teeth between the last upper molar and the bottom molar. Even more important was the fact that the miacids had relatively large brains. This development was due to the rapid evolution of herbivores, which forced the miacids

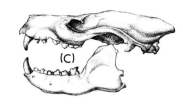

The skull of a creodont (above) shows the carnassials, the first upper molar and the second lower molar, here identified by (C).

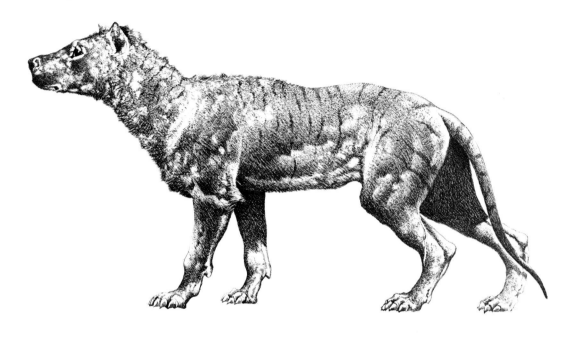

Hyaendodon, *left, like the creodont on the facing page, belonged to the hyaenodonts, but lived at a later period. These reconstructions show how the creodonts, similar to the carnivores of today, produced a great variety of forms.*

3 feet in length. The other two creodont families are the civetlike hyaenodonts and the wolverinelike oxyaeinids, both derived from the earlier arctocyonids. Both had specialized shearing teeth. *Sarkastodon* was nearly as large as the giant *Andrewsarchus*. *Patriofelis*, with hyenalike teeth, reached the size of a bear. The mesonychids diverged in that their teeth lacked shearing ability. The hyaenodonts survived longer than the other creodonts, into the late Eocene and early Oligocene, 35 million years ago. By then they had evolved into an animal proportioned like

to rely more on brain than on brawn for catching prey. From the miacids developed the two modern groups of land carnivores.

Later in the Oligocene, 25 to 35 million years ago, the miacids evolved into fissipeds such as the tree-living miacids and the *Cynodictis* and *Pseudocynodictis*, with a skeletal structure much like that of today's civet cats and weasels. Their short, spreading feet had five toes, apparently with retractile claws. With such characteristics, they can be placed at the ancestral base of almost any of the seven families of carnivores existing today.

Carnivores of Today

An example of fissiped teeth is shown at the right. Note that the canines are pink and the carnassials blue.

The wolf's teeth, as indicated by the letter "A", are representative of the canid family. Note that the premolars are not too sharp, and that the flat-crowned molars indicate a mixed, rather than strictly carnivorous diet.

The brown bear's teeth (B) represent a member of the ursid family. We see that the crowns of the molars have numerous rounded protuberances. The premolars are few and small and the carnassials are not specialized. All this indicates a decidedly omnivorous diet. It should be noted, however, that some species of bears are almost exclusively vegetarian.

The giant Panda is a member of the procyonid family. In his dentition (C) note how the premolars have come to resemble the molars, both of which serve a grinding function. While giant Panda's are almost entirely vegetarian, other procyonids are more omnivorous in their diet.

The polecat, a fierce predator and carnivore, is a member of the mustelid family. His teeth "D" indicate their use in tearing apart the prey (note the premolars and molars) The carnassials are also very conspicuous and highly developed.

All the carnivorous mammals that have survived to the present day are classed either as fissipeds or pinnipeds. All, as we have seen, can be considered descendants of the miacids. We know little about the beginnings of pinnipeds (seals, sea lions and walruses) because few fossils have been found. The only skeletal remains, dating from the Miocene, are a mere 20 million years old, but they show us that those early pinnipeds were much like their modern descendants.

During this period, mammals flourished and evolved as never before and never since. Living things began to look like the familiar forms we know today as the modern world began to take shape.

As we look at the two groups of modern carnivores, we can see that there are definite, very visible differences between them. The fissipeds are primarily land animals or, as in the case of the otters, equipped for semi-aquatic life. Therefore, fissipeds' limbs are best designed for walking, climbing, running and jumping. The pinnipeds are definitely made for a lifetime in the water, being equipped with flippers which are ideally suited for swimming.

Structural differences also include the following features. Fissipeds usually have long limbs, while the pinnipeds have short limbs and streamlined bodies enabling them to move about easily in the water. In contrast to the fissipeds, the pinnipeds have highly developed neck vertebrae, supporting arches for the shoulders and forelimbs, all related to the great force that the front limbs must produce while swimming. The teeth of the fissipeds are very specialized, while those of the pinnipeds tend to regress and occasionally reach a degree of marked uniformity. Since the pinnipeds are fish-eaters and do not have to tackle the tough hides of goat, antelope, elephant or rhino, this is not a surprising development.

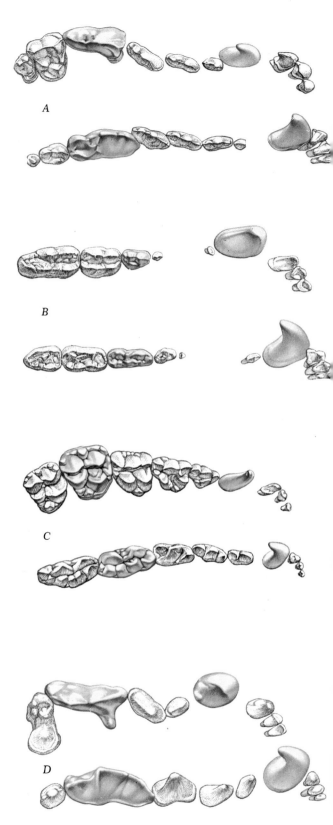

A

B

C

D

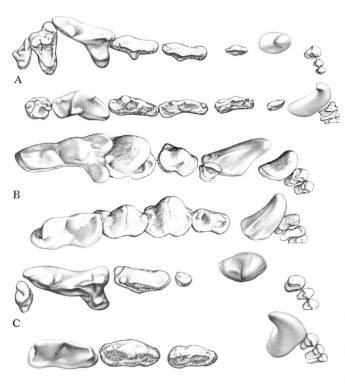

A

B

C

The Cloven-Footed Fissipeds

One of the earliest ways of distinguishing between the major groups within the order fissipeds was to consider the types of teeth and, even more, the way in which the foot rested on the ground. Certain animals, such as the bear, are *plantigrade*—that is, when they walk they put the sole and the heel of the foot on the ground. Other animals, such as the cat, are *digitigrade*, placing only the bottom side of the toes on the ground. The relative toughness of the skin on the lower surface of each animal's foot demonstrates the difference. This method was accepted by early naturalists as a highly important element in classification. However, it was later realized that this was a superficial way of distinguishing among the major groups of fissipeds and that greater anatomical differences would have to be used to separate them into proper subdivisions.

Shown at left are the teeth of some of the other families of land carnivores. In these groups the canines are shown in pink and the carnassials in blue.

The Viverrid family is here represented by a genet. While genets have the same number of teeth (A) as other canids, their structure is slightly different, adapted for carnivorous purposes.

The teeth of the spotted hyena (B), a member of the Hyaenid family are extremely strong. Note the well developed canines and carnassials, capable of crushing the most resistant bone.

The wildcat, a member of the felid family, shows teeth (C) that have been developed to the peak of perfection for a carnivore. Premolars and molars are fewer in number but strong and extremely efficient.

(lower left). Unlike the cats, the red fox has a fairly varied diet, with portions of fruit and berries accompanying its meat. Its canines and carnassials are nevertheless quite well-developed.

(lower right). Like all felids, the serval has a purely carnivorous diet, as is apparent from its sharp canines and highly developed carnassials.

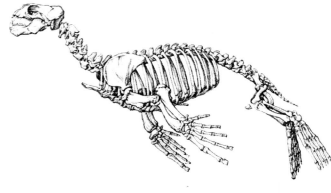

Shown on these two pages is a comparison of fissiped structure (opposite page) and pinniped structure (at right). The skeleton of the seal shows the remarkable shortness of the arm and forearm bones, and the thigh and lower leg, as compared to those of the dog on the page opposite. Also note the greater length of the phalanges in the eared seal, where they form flippers rather than paws.

Shown at the lower right are some samples of pinniped tooth structure. The canines are shown in pink.

The eared seal, a member of the Otariid family, has a basic diet of fish. To accommodate this food its teeth (A) are strong, sharp and of a uniform size.

The walrus, a representative of the Odobenid family, has flat teeth (B) for grinding mollusks and crustaceans. Only its canines, used for digging or defense, are longer and more powerful.

The earless seal belongs to the Phocid family. The uniformity of its teeth (C) is due to the basic diet of fish. Only the canines are well developed, being used to capture their prey.

For instance, the method of dividing the fissipeds into two large groups, the doglike canoids and the catlike feloids, resulted from observation of the *tympanic bulla,* a bony structure on the rear side of the skull that encloses part of the middle ear. This bony chamber is undivided in the canoids, but in the feloids it is separated into two portions by a bony wall. In addition, there are other, even more technical points of distinction.

The oldest fissipeds are closer to dogs than to cats. The canoids include the canids (dogs, wolves, foxes), the mustelids (weasels, martens, otters, skunks), the ursids (bears) and the procyonids (raccoons).

These animals have kept the long jaw that the miacids had as well as a large number of teeth. They have large snouts with a sense of smell that is superior among mammals.

The other group, the feloids, consists of the viverrids (civets, genets and mongooses), the hyaenids (hyenas) and the felids (all the cats). All these animals have shortened jaws, which gives them considerably better biting power.

While it is relatively easy to divide the living fissipeds into two natural groups on the basis of an analysis founded on the structure of the tympanic bulla, it becomes much more difficult to discover the exact patterns of kinship among the living families within the canoids and the feloids.

It is agreed by most zoologists that the miacids are the ancestors of both groups, but then the ancestry begins to diverge. The ursids and procyonids probably came from forms similar to the canids. Among the feloids, the viverridae and the hyaenids probably shared a common ancestor in Asia more than 12 million years ago. It appears that at the dawn of the Oligocene, about 32 million years ago, there were species that the classifiers have not been able to assign definitely. These could have been mustelids,

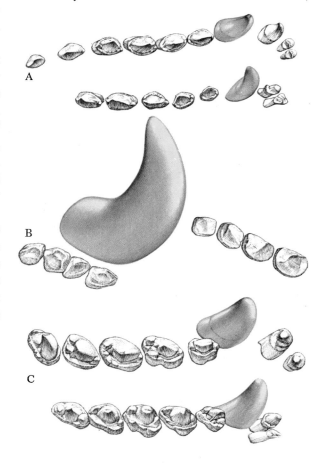

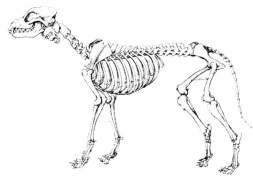

viverrids or felids. This shows that at that period of time, these groups were not clearly differentiated. While it is easy to assign an existing fissiped species to its proper "pigeon-hole," it is less feasible and often impossible to do so for the early members of this group.

The Teeth of Mammals

One of the most important ways of identifying fossil mammals is by means of their teeth, and so, before we go on to discuss the various families, let us see how mammalian teeth are described. This always follows the same formula, which takes into account only the teeth located on one side of the jaws. Because of what is known as bilateral symmetry, which means that each half of the body is identical to the other half, it follows that the teeth on either side must be the same too. Each tooth is indicated by an initial: I for incisor, C for canine, Pm for premolar and M for molar. Except for the canines, there is generally more than one of the other types of teeth in each side of the jaws. In order to identify any given

The big cats, as typified by this lazy lion, are the ultimate development for a life of hunting. Even in repose, this beast shows clearly the power of its muscular body, and the teeth, visible in its yawn, are frighteningly efficient.

19

(four altogether; two above and two below), or $C^{1/1}$; they have four premolars in each upper and lower jaw (16 altogether; eight upper and eight lower), or $Pm^{4/4}$; and finally two upper molars and three lower molars on each side (ten in all; four upper and six lower) or $M^{2/3}$. So, altogether the canids have 42 teeth, and their dental formula reads: $I^{3/3}, C^{1/1}, Pm^{4/4}$ and $M^{2/3} = 42$.

The Canids—Dogs, Wolves and Foxes

The canids constitute a very homogeneous family, distributed throughout almost the entire world with the exception of New Zealand, New Guinea, Madagascar, Formosa, the Antilles and the Celebes. This distribution, however, excludes the domestic dog, which has followed man everywhere and is found universally today.

Of a sociable nature, the canids commonly live and hunt in packs, relying on team effort to track and take their quarry.

The most ancient forms date back to the Eocene, when a species, the *Procynodictis*, lived in North America. It was in the Miocene, however, that this group reached its peak, branching out into many forms, most of which became extinct well before recent times. One interesting exception that long

(above). The diagonal lines show the position of land masses that emerged during the Paleocene period between southeast Asia and Australia. The absence of any link between these continents since that time has resulted in profound differences in the fauna of these two regions.

Beneath the closed lips of the wolf (shown above right) are the efficient teeth illustrated below. The teeth are identified: I for incisor, C for canine, PM for premolar and M for molar. The upper jaw is seen from underneath; the lower jaw in profile. The carnassials are shown in red.

tooth, a sequential numbering system is used. For the maxillary teeth, the tooth initial is followed by a number above; for the mandible, the number goes below. The numbers begin with the tooth closest to the plane of symmetry (the plane that divides the body into equal halves). Thus the first upper incisor is I^1 and the first lower incisor is I_1. The successive incisors are, respectively, I^2 and I_2. When reference is made to the dental formula as a whole, the symbols of the various teeth will be followed by fractions in which the numerator refers to the number of that kind of tooth in the half-maxillary, and the denominator refers to its number in the half-mandible.

Using a specific example, the canids generally have three incisors in each half of each jaw (twelve altogther; six above and six below) and so we use the code $I^{3/3}$; they have one upper and one lower canine on each side

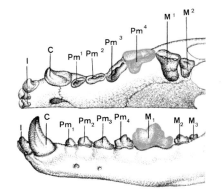

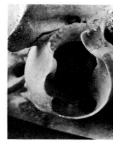

puzzled scientists is the dingo, the wild dog of Australia, because it is the only placental carnivore on a continent of meat-eating marsupials. Most likely, the dingo is an early breed of domestic dog brought to Australia by primitive man from the southeastern part of Asia. This might have happened about 20,000 years ago. Now the dingo runs wild, living and hunting in packs and feeding on kangaroo meat. The pups are sometimes tamed for hunting by the aborigines, today's survivors of the Stone Age.

Aside from dogs, wolves and foxes, the canids include coyotes and jackals, the maned wolf of South America and the raccoon-dog groups which are almost worldwide in range.

The Ursids—the Bears

Today bears are found in a large part of the Northern Hemisphere and in some areas of the Southern Hemisphere (see map, p. 23). Bears, which are plantigrade, have flattened molars suitable for grinding up many different kinds of food, rather than just meat. The bear has no carnassials and uses its canines as both offensive and defensive tools. The number of teeth is not much different from that of the canids, but often some premolars or molars are lacking. Generally, it is Pm^2 and Pm_2 that are not present or, if they do

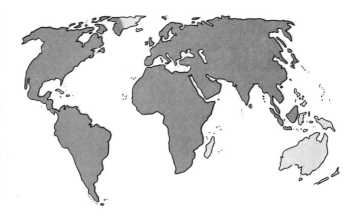

exist, are so small and useless that they disappear as soon as the cub has been weaned and has begun to use its teeth to get its own food.

Bears appeared in the Miocene, although some forms of Oligocene carnivores, *Cynodon* and *Cynodictis*, might perhaps be related to the bears of the present. The direct ancestor of the bear was probably *Ursavus*, which has been found fossilized in Bavaria in the Lower Miocene; this genus already showed the reduced premolars, a feature just mentioned.

The most famous fossil bear is the giant cave bear. Its remains have been found in many areas, such as caves and in rocky cliffs. There are a variety of reasons why

The brown areas of the map (above) show the distribution of the Canidae, except for the domestic dog, inasmuch as its distribution is the same as man's. The only carnivore in Australia is the dingo, a dog taken there by prehistoric man; it subsequently reverted to the wild state. Many kinds of dogs have been bred by man for various purposes. Most have been selected on the basis of hunting ability, as evidenced by the two dogs shown below.

At the bottom of the page opposite, to the right of the wolf's teeth, is shown the structure which differentiates the two basic groups of carnivores, the canoids and the feloids. This is the tympanic bulla, in the middle ear region of the skull. At top, in a canoid, it is undivided; the bottom picture shows the same structure, but with a partition, as it is found in the feloids.

these remains are so numerous. In some instances bones were carried by swift flowing flood waters, depositing them in the crevices that led to underground chambers. The cave bears probably found shelter in these great natural vaults in which they died. We can assume that the men who sometimes lived in these caves or who had transformed them into places of worship brought in the remains of these bears to be sacrificed during their religious ceremonies.

In spite of its huge canines, its great size and its fierce appearance, the cave bear may be described as the least carnivorous of all the bears. From the functional point of view, its molar teeth were not very different from those of herbivores. Even the carnassial was not specialized, but formed a part of the entire large chewing complex.

The Procyonids—Raccoons, Coatis and Pandas

The procyonids include a number of plantigrade or semiplantigrade carnivores that for some time were placed in the bear family because of those characteristics. Most of the species (raccoons, the intelligent coatis, the monkeylike kinkajous and olingos, the cacomistles or ring-tailed cats) live in North and South America, including the Bahamas but excluding the Antilles (see map). Two species, the lesser panda and the giant panda, live astride the border of India and China.

In the giant panda, a form considered by some authorities to be very close to the bears, the dental formula differs from that of the bears by the existence of only three premolars in the mandible and a reduction in size, or even a lack of, Pm^1. In the other existing genera, the molars are even fewer in number (two upper and two lower). The history of the procyonids is difficult to ascertain, although some contend that they derive from primitive, tree-dwelling carnivores that produced both this group and the canids. Others believe that there is a kinship, which perhaps is more logical, between the ursids and the procyonids. In any event, it is known that the ancestors of the Procyonidae lived in Europe and Asia during the Miocene.

The procyonids, although extremely dissimilar as a group, include types whose char-

The map at the lower left indicates the area of distribution of the Ursidae, shown in green. The range of prehistoric ursids was far greater at that time than in the present day. Bears, like the one shown below, are becoming so rare that, in certain areas, they are put under government protection.

(opposite page). An American bear exhibits its long tongue, with which it can "clean out" the cells of honeycombs. It is especially fond of honey. In addition to this black bear, the kodiak (below) and the grizzly also live in North America.

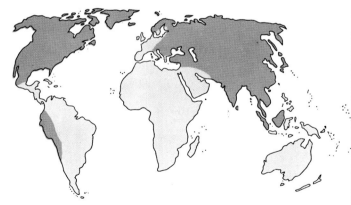

A group of raccoons at the water's edge exemplifies the curious habit these creatures have of washing everything that comes into their possession, especially their food. They live in Central and North America.

Brown areas are those inhabited by the Procyonidae. Their range of distribution is discontinuous: some live in the Western Hemisphere, while others are limited to a restricted area of the Far East. Fossil procyonids have also been found in Europe.

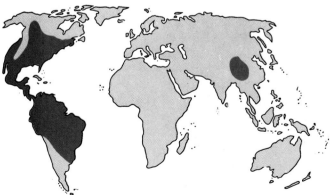

acteristics, for the most part, are alike. In essence, what unites them is much more important than what differentiates them. In this group, the molars often lose their characteristic carnivorous appearance and grow to resemble the teeth of a specialized herbivore. Yet even in these herbivorous carnivores, such as the giant panda, the diet occasionally includes rodents and insects.

The Mustelids—Weasels, Badgers, Otters and Skunks

The mustelids include many species of diverse animals of small and medium size. They are almost worldwide in distribution, except for Australia, New Guinea, New Zealand, Madagascar and the Antilles (see map). Generally, these animals prey on small and medium-sized birds and mammals, and they do not really compete with the large canids and felids. The mustelids have elegant bodies. Fearless by nature, they track their prey into even the most hidden of refuges. Only someone who has watched a

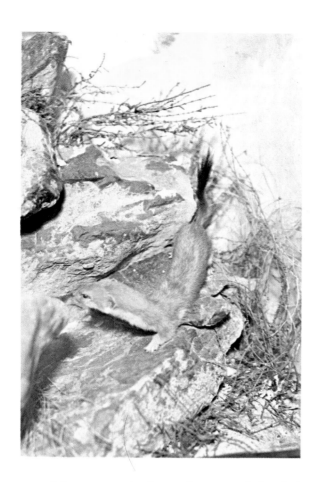

weasel hunt or raised a polecat or defended a chickenhouse against martens can grasp the capacity of the mustelids for aggressiveness and savagery.

The dental formula of these animals varies; the customary three incisors and the canines are followed by premolars, which range from two to four on each side of both the upper and lower jaws, and the molars, which are always single on each side of the maxillary and which may be single or double on each side of the mandible.

Often the mustelids have glands around the anus capable of emitting special odors, which serve as a mating signal. More often, however, the animal employs these glands to mark off its territory by sprinkling the ground with their secretions. The odor then serves as a warning to a male of the same species; he knows that if he enters the scented area he will have to fight its occupant. This is a primitive but frequently used means of communicating "land ownership," or territoriality, in the world of mammals.

To date, the origins of the mustelids have not been clarified. The miacid fissiped *Cynodictis* seems to be the first certain ancestor. The Oligocene forms cannot be accurately defined and, as already noted, there seems to be no clear distinction among mustelids, felids and viverrids from that time.

In some early types, the second upper molar is still present, although it is definitely of musteline type; in others, the second molar has diappeared.

In connection with the living mustelids, it is interesting to observe the phenomenon of changing coat color in several species of weasel. The classic example is that of the ermine, whose coat is brown in summer and turns white, with a black-tipped tail, in winter. Such a change provides a camouflage

The three representative mustelids shown above are the weasel, the polecat and the marten.

The European weasel, as shown at left, is distinguished by its small size and serpentine body.

The red areas of the map below indicate those inhabited by the Mustelidae. Their tremendous range of distribution, like those of all carnivores, excludes Australia. They have, however, been recently introduced to that continent for the purpose of exterminating harmful rodents.

25

Orange areas, shown in the map below, are those inhabited by the Hyaenidae. While their territory at present is very limited, in past geological ages they could be found in many parts of Europe and Asia.

A spotted hyena and a flock of busy vultures are shown around a carcass. In the search for food, the hyena often relies on its very sharp sense of smell or goes where it sees gatherings of vultures.

that remains effective with the changing seasons, and is by no means exclusive to the ermine. It is found among other mammals as well, for example the white fox and the Arctic hare.

The small size of these animals occasionally leads to the use of weapons for survival

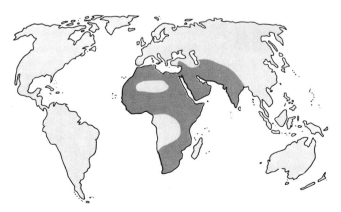

that are different from the usual tooth-and-claw methods. A well known example is the skunk, which is capable of spraying its enemy with an overwhelmingly scented potion from its perianal glands. Another unusual defense is that of the badger which, when cornered by an enemy, has been known to roll itself off a cliff.

The Viverrids—Civets, Genets and Mongooses

The modern viverrids live exclusively in the Old World and do not exist at all in the Americas, Australia or New Zealand. Only in Europe do the viverrids extend beyond a latitude of 40° north, being found in Spain and some parts of southern France.

Viverrids are small and medium-sized carnivores characterized by a dental structure consisting of 40 teeth ($I^{3/3}$, $C^{1/1}$, $Pm^{4/4}$ and $M^{2/2}$). Occasionally, some of the premolars are absent. It is easy to distinguish the skull of a viverrid from that of a mustelid because, in modern mustelids, the upper molars are always represented by a single tooth, while in the viverrids there are two (the exception being the civetlike fossa of Madagascar). As has already been mentioned, the mustelids and the viverrids probably have a common ancestor. Furthermore, some of the viverrids appear to be related to the felids. The fossa of Madagascar, for example, has claws that can be retracted and a rounded skull, both features that it shares with the cats. As always in these instances, it is hard to decide whether the shared characteristics are due to direct relationship or have been independently acquired by both groups.

The viverrids, which are predominantly but not exclusively carnivorous, are divided into five major and one minor grouping. These are the civets, the mongooses, the palm civets, the Asiatic palm civets, the Malagasy mongooses and the fossa.

The Hyaenids—the Hyenas

The hyaenids have a common ancestry with the viverrids, even though they look entirely different. Hyenas closely resemble large, awkward-looking dogs. Today, hyenas are limited to Africa, part of Asia Minor, certain regions southeast of the Caspian Sea, Arabia and India. Their dental formula is $I^{3/3}$, $C^{1/1}$, $Pm^{3-4/3}$ and $M^{1/1}$.

Ictitherium, now extinct and known only from fossil remains that are about 10 million years old, possessed characteristics that place it somewhere between viverrids and hyaenids. These seem to have evolved into large carnivores specializing in scavenging and feeding upon the carcasses of big game. The transition from *Ictitherium* to forms close to living species was relatively swift and there has been little evolutionary change since.

The areas inhabited by the Viverridae are shown in violet on the map at left. Typical of the Old World, the viverrids are the only carnivores found in Madagascar and the Celebes. They have, however, recently been imported to some parts of the New World.

The **Aardwolf** (*Proteles cristatus*) is the sole species in its genus. Native to South Africa, it looks like a small, striped hyena. Its habitat is sandy plain or bush, its diet includes carrion and white ants.

Notwithstanding its small size, the dwarf mongoose, shown below, is very aggressive when it comes to killing snakes.

The Felids—the Cats

Regions inhabited by the Felidae are shown in black on the map below. Just as we omitted the domestic dog from our discussion of the Canidae, we here leave aside the domestic cat, which has shared man's adventures everywhere in the world. The extreme Arctic or Antarctic are the only two areas where felids are not found.

In the felids, the carnivores reached an evolutionary peak. So well were they adapted to the demands of their environment that henceforth they were able to branch out into a wide variety of almost uniform types.

The early history of the felids, like that of the viverrids and mustelids, is for the most part, lost. The first forms appeared between two clearly identifiable lines, one represented by animals having especially long upper canines, and the other group by animals with relatively "normal" canines. The former went even further in their "exaggerated" canine development and culminated in the saber-toothed "tigers" of later times. The latter retained more or less the same proportion of canine teeth into the present.

Today the felids are present all over the

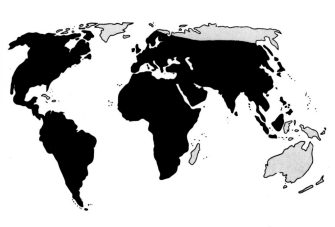

The leopard (right) not only uses his tree as a dining room, but also retreats into its branches to rest.

the end of the Eocene and the beginning of the Oligocene in the drier areas of the Northern Hemisphere.

Two major groups of felids are recognized. The first group is represented by the now extinct saber-toothed cats, which are known from the Oligocene to the Pleistocene; the second group is that of the true cats, the felines, also known since the Oligocene. The felines are the group to which all living felids belong.

From the beginning, the felids fell into

world (see map), with the exception of Australia, New Zealand, Madagascar, Iceland, the extreme Arctic regions, the Antilles, the Celebes and New Guinea.

The felids are characterized by a harmony of body parts unequaled among mammals and directed toward a single end, the hunt. Because its prey is wary and able to perceive danger, the cat body is supple and lithe, permitting a silent approach; once within range, however, the cat replaces stealth with speed, moving very quickly toward its victim. The parts of the body that have changed to the greatest extent from the original shrewlike pattern are the skull (including the teeth) and the limbs. The muscles are well developed, the strongest being in the back, the hind legs (which give the impulse for leaping) and the shoulders and neck (used for holding down prey and in biting).

Compared to mammals as a group, cats are

$I^{3/3}$, $C^{1/1}$, $Pm^{3/2}$ and $M^{1/1}$, consisting of a total of 30 teeth. In the fossil *Smilodon*, the giant Ice Age saber tooth, and in the saber-toothed cats generally, the premolars were reduced in number. The cat's incisor teeth are of little help in hunting or feeding and are used, rather, for grooming the fur. The canines, however, are very important. They, along with the claws, are the weapons used in the kill. They are also used in ripping and tear-

Although lions are fierce hunters, they make gentle, affectionate parents, taking great pains in the protection and education of their young. After their naps, these cubs are likely to receive a hunting lesson from their mother.

reasonably bright. They have very keen senses, possessing large and well developed eyes, ears and noses. Their brains are large, with the higher centers dominant. As with all mammals, however, innate patterns of behavior underlie many cat activities, although learning from experience also plays an important role.

The teeth of the felids are specialized for the killing and dismemberment of prey, an activity in which they are helped by short, strong jaws. The typical dental formula is

ing the flesh of the prey after the kill has been made. Then the carnassial teeth cut through the pieces of meat like a pair of shears, the cat finally swallowing small chunks whole.

Compared to most mammals, cats have superior vision, and although relatively color-blind, they are able to see quite well both in daylight and darkness. Their ability to judge distance is also excellent, and this is an important factor when a cat is preparing to pounce on its prey.

Most cats have beautiful coats, but to the cat the importance of its coat lies in its ability to provide camouflaging. As a stealthy hunter, the cat must approach its prey without being noticed. To this end nature has provided the cat family with coats of many shades and many different designs. Cats that hunt in the open have coats of various shades of brown, blending in with surroundings. Cats that hunt in forested areas have spots or stripes, and these blend with the shadows cast by the leaves and foliage.

Pinnipeds—Flippered Mammals of the Seas

It is difficult to pick out the group or groups of carnivores that gave rise to the flippered pinnipeds. There is much physical evidence pointing to a close relationship between fissipeds and pinnipeds, both groups having a common ancestor, but whether the pinnipeds have their origin among the miacids or in an already separate group of fissipeds is difficult to decide. The pinnipeds are so different from other carnivores that they are generally considered to be a distinct suborder.

The pinnipeds are divided into three groups: the seals with ears (Otariidae), the walruses (Odobenidae) and the seals without ears (Phocidae). The pinnipeds, as a whole, are found in virtually all the world's seas, but they seem to prefer cold-water zones. Seals are not exclusively fish-eaters. Many of them also eat sea birds, other seals, shellfish and other marine life.

The Otariidae — Fur Seals and Sea Lions

Seals with ears have hind flippers that can be rotated forward in a way that makes it possible to travel on land. Aside from these hind flippers, the eared seals can also be recognized by their slender profile and, as is indicated by their name, the presence of small external ears which are completely lacking in the other pinnipeds. Species of this family are found along the coasts in both the northern and southern hemispheres, although more species are found in the latter.

Adult male sea lions range from 6 to 7 feet in length and weigh between 400 and 700 pounds; females are about 5 feet long and weigh between 75 and 125 pounds. Fe-

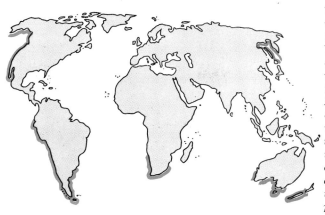

The blue areas on the map opposite are those inhabited by the Otaridae. While they flourish predominantly in southern waters, they are also found in the Northern Hemisphere. The Phocidae dominate in northern waters, with a few species in the south. Phocids are to be found on all coasts of the world including the equatorial regions, where the otariids are completely lacking.

males give birth to a single pup, and they are bred again a few days after giving birth; thus they are almost always pregnant. Cows can have pups until the age of 21, which is about their average lifespan.

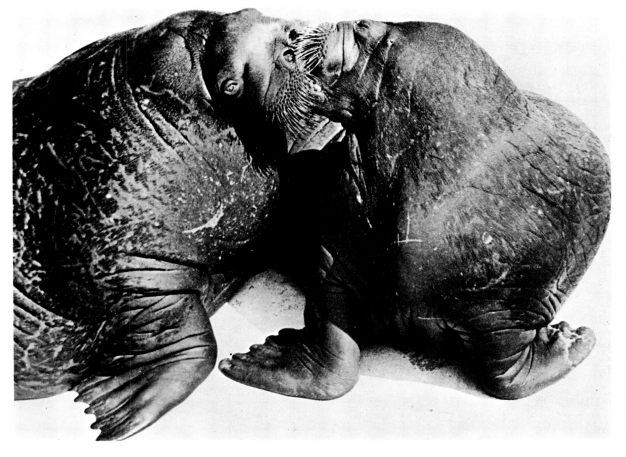

The two devoted walruses at left belong to the family Odobenidae. Like the California sea lion of the family Otariidae (opposite page), they can rotate their rear flippers forward in such a way as to permit them to hunch themselves forward on land—a primitive prelude to walking.

31

seal

sea lion

The sea lion (above) is immediately distinguishable from the seal (top of page) by its ability to flex its hind flippers forward. But the basic distinguishing characteristic is the sea lion's possession of external ears, which the seal lacks.

The Odobenidae— the Walruses

Walruses are large and stout—as much as 12 feet in length and 1½ tons in weight—with a small head and a square muzzle. Their most distinguishing characteristic is the appearance of large tusks, formed by the elongation of the upper canines. The other teeth are small pegs, suitable for crushing the mollusks which are the walruses' principal source of food.

Two subspecies of walrus are recognized —*Odobenus rosmarus rosmarus*, the Atlantic walrus, and *Odobenus rosmarus divergens*, the Pacific walrus. Their ranges approach each other closely near Severnaya Zemla in the far northern seas, but they have not been known to interbreed. In modern times they have rarely been known to venture further south than Iceland or the Bering Sea; they are distinctly northern animals, inhabiting coastal areas and ice floes near the land. They travel in herds, sometimes more than 100 strong, emitting loud cries. The female, about two-thirds the size of the male, carries her young for about eleven months and nurses her babies for about two years. The females are sexually mature at five years, the males when they are six years old.

The Phocidae— the Earless Seals

This family is characterized by hind flippers that cannot move forward and are of no use in land travel. These seals are worldwide in distribution, there being cold-water seals, warm-water seals and even a freshwater seal, the Baikal seal (*Pusa sibirica*), named for the lake in which it lives.

The dentition of these particular seals is variable. Adults average about 5 feet in length and weigh between 125 and 300 pounds. Gestation is slightly over nine months, and the pup is weaned at about six weeks; the average lifespan is about 15 years.

The true origins of the seals are still unknown. Some believe that they are descendants of the creodonts of the *Oxyaenid* group; others link them with the mustelids of the otter group, while still others trace seals, par-

The hair seal (left) lives on the northern coasts of the Atlantic Ocean from Greenland to Portugal, along the entire northern coast of Asia, and on the North American coast of the Pacific. These seals always remain close to the shore and rarely venture into the open sea.

ticularly the eared seals, back to ancestral forms of bear. Because of the lack of adequate fossil evidence, this problem of origin seems destined to go unsolved.

These seals are highly adapted for life in the water. Their name derives from the fact that they lack an external ear. Body and limbs are covered with a coat of short, coarse hair, with no undercoating of fur. Yet they breed and bear their young on land—and it is a curious fact that their babies must be taught to swim, a duty which usually falls to the mother, who prods them onward in the learning process despite the crashing seas of northern latitudes. Valued for their hides and their oil, they are relentlessly hunted.

Sea lions like these pictured at the left are highly gregarious during the breeding season, when they come to rocky islands or isolated coastal areas to bear and rear their young.

The Viverrids—Bearers of Musk

The Viverridae have the largest number of species of any carnivorous family, yet little is known about this important group because of their primarily nocturnal habits, timidity and prudence. On the other hand, there are some species that are quite famous. Rikki-tikki-tavi in Rudyard Kipling's *Indian Tales* was the unforgettable mongoose who subdued cobras, and the Oriental civet was known in antiquity for the supposed medicinal quality of the secretion from its anal glands. Today *civet*, as this secretion is called, is used in the making of perfume.

The ancestors of the Viverridae are not well known. A few fossil genera, such as *Ictitherium* of the Miocene epoch, testify to the relationship of the hyaenids and viverrids, but there is no material from any earlier deposits that gives any real clues to the exact ancestry of the two families.

Today the group is represented by six subfamilies, divided into 37 genera, totaling some 80 species, all of which are found only in the Old World (Asia, Africa, Europe and

Madagascar). Africa has the greatest number of species, while Europe has only two. Some of the viverrids have been introduced into various countries by man in an attempt to control poisonous snakes and rodents. Examples are: the masked palm civet (*Paguma*), introduced into Japan, and the mongoose (*Herpestes*) into Hawaii and the West Indies. Often these viverrids multiply to the point of becoming excessive, and they begin to destroy poultry and to undermine the natural faunal balance of the areas into which they have been introduced.

The skull of the Madagascar fossa is seen in profile (left) and frontally (below) with the mouth open so that the tooth structure can be clearly seen. In each half of both upper and lower jaws, the fossa has three incisors, one canine, three premolars, and one molar. The function of the carnassial teeth is added to by the shearing action of the third upper premolar. This is an exceptionally powerful dentition.

General Characteristics

Generally, viverrids have long, slender bodies and short limbs that may be either plantigrade or digitigrade. Their total length varies from 1 to 6 feet, their weight from 1 pound (the dwarf mongoose) to 30 pounds (the binturong). The coat varies a great deal, but it is frequently heavily speckled. They usually have long tails with alternating rings of light and dark fur. In many viverrids the muzzle strongly resembles that of a cat, so much so in the case of the fossa (*Cryptoprocta*) that this animal is still classified by some among the felids.

The viverrids have either five toes on all their feet or five on the forefeet and four on the hind feet, with a few species that have four toes on all feet. In many species the claws are retractile. The habitat is quite

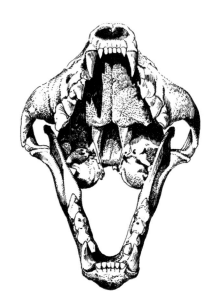

The animal on the opposite page is a suricate, a member of the family Viverridae. Suricates live only in southern Africa, in burrows or rock crevices. Sitting up on their haunches and basking in the sun is one of their favorite ways of passing that part of their time which is not consumed in hunting for insects, snakes, birds and small mammals.

varied, the same species often being found in different environments. Although found mostly in forests, they can also be seen in brush and grassland. Some forms take refuge in dens dug in the earth, others find shelter inside inhabited buildings or in drainage pipes. Generally, the viverrids lead solitary lives or travel in pairs; only in rare cases do they gather in groups. Members of the genera *Cynictis* and *Suricata*, generally called meerkats, live in colonies in subterranean dens, much as certain rodents do—a very unusual practice for animals with carnivorous habits. Some viverrids are adept at climbing trees, where they spend a good part of their lives; others prefer the water and swim with great ease.

Mainly carnivorous, some viverrids are plant-eaters as well, and the palm civets eat mostly fruit. The mongooses are ground hunters and will attack almost any animal that is not too large to handle. The hunting tactics of the group, as a whole, are rather simple. The viverrids attack small vertebrates either on the ground or in trees. They also like insects. They have excellent eyes, ears and noses, and even though they are not combative, they will fight well when cornered. They often emit an extremely unpleasant odor from their anal scent glands as a defensive device.

Usually the viverrids reproduce in the spring and summer, but in most species not much is known of their reproductive habits. It is known that the period of pregnancy for the ichneumon (a kind of mongoose) is about 60 days, after which the female gives birth to from one to six young; these young are born covered with fur but still blind.

The family is generally divided into six groups called subfamilies.

The Viverrines—Civets, Genets and Linsangs

The subfamily Viverrinae is divided into two "tribes." First there are the true viverrines, and these include the six genera that are neither arboreal nor burrowing. They are characterized by their short, semiretractile

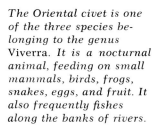

The Oriental civet is one of the three species belonging to the genus Viverra. *It is a nocturnal animal, feeding on small mammals, birds, frogs, snakes, eggs, and fruit. It also frequently fishes along the banks of rivers.*

claws, their typical viverrid teeth and the presence of anal scent glands. The other "tribe" consists of the Oriental linsangs (all in the genus *Poionodon*). These have retractile claws and lack anal scent glands; their dental structure is characterized by the absence of the second upper molars.

The Oriental Civets, which comprise the three species within the genus *Viverra*, are found in southern Asia. Adults weigh between 15 and 25 pounds; they are covered with long fur, particularly during the cold season. Along the back, the hair grows longer than elsewhere and forms a modest crest or mane. The coat is gray or brown, with varied markings of a different color; the sides of the neck and the throat are striped black and white. In two species of this genus—*Viverra zibetha* and *Viverra tangalunga*—the third and fourth toes of the front paws do not have lobes of skin to protect the retractile claws.

The civets generally lead a fairly solitary and nocturnal life. By day they hide and sleep in the forest or dense brush, venturing out at nightfall for food.

While civets are very proficient at climbing trees, they generally hunt on the ground, stalking and killing smaller mammals, birds, snakes, frogs and insects. They will also eat eggs, fruit, roots and fish.

After mating the female will generally give birth to from one to four young. This takes place in a hollow dug in the soft earth or made in the dense undergrowth.

The civets are the closest of the viverrines to cats, but they have a more slender appearance and a sharper head. They are 1½ to 2 feet in length, with a tail about the same length as the body.

The African Civet is the sole species of the genus *Civettictis* and is technically known as *C. civetta*. It lives in the forest and plains of Africa from Senegal in the west to Somalia in the east throughout South Africa. It may attain a fairly large size, sometimes as much as 4 feet. It is covered with a beautiful black coat with white or yellowish

The African civet at the lower left, like many other viverrids, has special glands in the anal region, the secretions of which it uses to mark out its territory. Commercially, this product is used to "fix" the scent in some perfumes.

The lesser Oriental civet, (below), which is smaller than the other representatives of the genus Viverra, *lives a solitary life, hunting mainly during the nocturnal hours.*

The common mongoose is active day or night in search for food. Its diet frequently includes the meat of such poisonous snakes as the cobra.

stripes and spots. The long, thick hair becomes thicker in the tail; a series of erect hairs along the back form a crest. The African civet has a glandular sac—a musk sac —which discharges through a longitudinal fissure in the anal region. The paws have five toes, and the soles of the feet are covered with hair.

The African civet is small-headed and narrow, with long hind legs. A night animal, it hides during the day in the thick forest or underbrush. It is raised in Ethiopia for its "civet," or musk. This substance, which looks like rancid butter, is obtained from the animals with a special tool formed like a long-handled teaspoon.

In most instances, this civet does not reproduce in captivity. (In its natural environment, it normally gives birth to two or three young twice a year.) The diet of the African civet is very similar to that of the other viverrids. However, it also feeds on cornstalk tops, fruits and tubers.

The Lesser Oriental Civet (*Viverricula indica*) is the only representative of its genus. It inhabits southern India, southeast Asia and southern China. It was brought into Socotra, the Comoro Islands and Madagascar, probably for the production of "civet."

This animal differs from species belonging to the genus *Viverra* not only because of

The African linsang (at left) lives only in western Africa and on the island of Fernando Po. It is a forest animal that hunts by night and during the day rests in tangled vines.

its smaller size (it never weighs more than 9 pounds) but also because of its narrower forehead and more closely placed ears; it also lacks the crest on its back.

These civets also lead a solitary existence, being rarely encountered in pairs. They are nocturnal, resting or looking for food during the day only where vegetation is thick. They feed on small invertebrates, insects, larvae, fruit and roots. The female gives birth to two to five young.

The Genets (genus *Genetta*, nine species) are found almost exclusively in Africa (except for the Sahara); one species lives in Israel, Arabia and southwestern Europe.

These animals are particularly long and agile, with tails almost as long as their bodies. There is a variety in the pattern of the coat but all have stripes of dark spots on lighter ground, light spots underneath the eyes, a black back crest and light and dark rings on the tail.

Genets live in forests or areas of thick vegetation. They are mostly tree dwellers. They rest during the day, coming out at night to hunt birds, eggs, small mammals, reptiles and invertebrates. They also raid henhouses.

Genets also emit a fluid from the anal glands that has a musty smell. *Genetta genetta*, the only species of this genus that appears in Europe, is generally unaggressive and is quite shy. The African species usually give birth to two or three young twice a year, in the spring and fall. These animals have been known to live up to 34 years in zoos.

The Congo Water Civet (*Osbornictis piscivora*) is found in the Congo forests. It was first discovered in 1916, and it is unlike anything else known. It has never been caught alive and is described only from museum specimens. The coat has no markings and the tail has no rings. Adults measure about 3 feet, one-third of which is tail. The animal has reddish-brown fur, a black tail and light markings on its head. It has weak teeth—a

reflection of its fish diet—and apparently lives mainly in the water.

The African Linsang (*Poiana richardsoni*) is also the only one of its kind. The genus name is derived from that of the Portuguese explorer Fernando Po.

The animal is about 2½ feet long and is covered with a rusty yellow-gray coat and irregularly arranged spots; it has dark-brown or black rings on its tail. Some individuals of this species have alternating wide and narrow rings.

Decidedly omnivorous, the oyan, as it is sometimes called, feeds on both animals and vegetables. It builds large, round nests out of vegetable material for a shelter at night.

The genet at right feeds on small birds, eggs, small mammals, and invertebrates. It lives a mainly nocturnal life.

Small groups of individual animals will take refuge in the nest for several nights. Little is known about the habits of this linsang.

The Oriental Linsangs (genus *Prionodon*) comprise two species—the striped linsang (*Prionodon linsang*), which inhabits Tenasserim, Sumatra, Java and Borneo, and the spotted linsang (*Prionodon pardicolor*), which lives in Nepal, Assam, North Burma and Indochina. Both these forms have beautiful marked coats and slender shapes; they are about 2½ feet long, half of which is the tail. They generally weigh less than 2½ pounds. They spend more time on the ground, stalking birds, lizards and frogs, than do genets.

The oriental linsangs have retractile claws, and their rear paws have special sheaths to accommodate them. The skin of the rear paws forms characteristic protective lobes. According to the little information we have, these linsangs emit no odor, they hunt at night, they build nests in hollow trees above ground level.

Palm Civets and Binturongs

Six genera go to make up a group which includes the African palm civets, with one genus, *Nandinia*; the small-toothed palm civets (Asiatic), with one genus, *Arctogalidia*; and the true palm civets, including the binturong, with four genera (*Paradoxurus, Paguma, Macrogalidia* and *Arctictis*) distributed in southeast Asia and the Indo-Malay region. The latter are identified by raised areas of hard skin which are joined at the base of the third and fourth toes of the rear paws; in *Arctogalidia* these callosities are separate. The teeth pattern in the true palm civets is typically viverrid, and scent glands are present in both males and females.

The African Palm Civet (*Nandinia binotata*) is the only species of the genus *Nandinia*. It has short, very thick, coarse fur and short legs. It is a climber rather than a jumper. Basically brown, it has dark spots throughout and two discernible white spots on the shoulders. Its tail is even longer than its body. The soles of the feet are without any hair and show a characteristic surface, almost as though they were composed of many granules. The ani-

The genet shown at lower left returns each morning to the same tree for shelter throughout the sultry daytime hours.

The cranium of the African linsang (left) is very long. The dentition is typically carnivorous without, however, reaching the stage of specialization that it does in the Felids.

mal is mainly active during the night, feeding on fruits, mammals and small birds. The natives keep it inside their houses to eliminate rodents and cockroaches. Its area of distribution covers central and southern Africa and Fernando Po.

The Celebes Palm Civet (*Macrogalidia musschenbroecki*), the only species of its genus, is now an exceedingly rare animal confined to the northeastern part of Celebes Island. At one time it was found throughout the island, as fossil remains in the southern part testify.

The animal is about 3 feet long, with a chestnut-colored coat; its stripes are not very distinct, and it has several rings on its tail. Its habits are virtually unknown. It feeds on rats and fruits and is very fond of papaya.

(above) The palm civet, also known as the musang, lives in southeast Asia and on the Celebes.

(below) The masked palm civet is named for the characteristic mask pattern on its face.

(upper right) The binturong is the only carnivore, aside from the kinkajou (a procyonid), with a prehensile tail.

The Masked Palm Civet (*Paguma larvata*) is the sole species of the genus Paguma. It inhabits southeastern China, Taiwan, Hainan, the Malay Peninsula and Burma and was recently introduced into Japan. Measuring about 4 feet in length, it weighs about 10 pounds. It has a tawny-gray or reddish coat without any spots or stripes except for a few white markings on the head.

The habits of this species are not well known. Found chiefly in forest land, it is a tree-dweller and eats plants as well as fish. While it effectively destroys rats, it does not attack henhouses. The masked palm civet also has very potent scent glands. It is extremely powerful, killing animals double its size but also eating fruits, insects and fish. The female gives birth to three or four young in the hollows of trees.

The Palm Civets or Musangs of the genus *Paradoxurus* include three species: *P. jerdoni*, inhabiting southern India; *P. zeylonensis*, living in Ceylon; and *P. hermaphroditus*, a native of southern Asia from Ceylon and India to China, the Philippines, Malaysia and some Pacific Islands.

These animals measure about 4 feet in length and weigh about 5 pounds. They have a grayish or brown coat, the color of which is more or less marked by long, black protective hairs, sometimes with stripes along the back or spots along the flanks. A white stripe crosses the forehead and white markings appear under the eyes. In the first two species mentioned above, the hairs on the neck grow from the shoulders toward the head; in *P. hermaphroditus* the hairs grow from the head toward the tail.

Musangs are nocturnal animals and good climbers, usually living in trees or in thick underbrush. They frequently appear in the vicinity of human dwellings, probably attracted by the presence of rodents; they seek refuge in drainage canals or under straw roofs. They essentially feed on small-sized vertebrates, insects, fruits and seeds. Especially fond of palm juice, or toddy, they owe their common name "toddy cat" to this characteristic. All three species, but especially *P. hermaphroditus*, can emit a powerful odor from their anal glands, a tactic that they

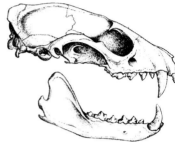

The African palm civet (left) is kept as a domestic pet because it catches rodents and insects.

Compared to most viverrids, which have an elongated nose, the cranium of the African palm civet (below) shows a rather short one.

employ against predators when they have exhausted every other recourse. The female musang gives birth to two to four young.

The Small-toothed Palm Civet (*Arctogalidia trivirgata*) is the only species of its genus. It can be found in southeast Asia and the Malay Archipelago. Weighing about 4 pounds, it measures 3½ feet from nose to tail. Its fur is grayish-brown, darker about the head, with the paws and tail tip being dark brown. A white stripe divides the face in half, and the underside of the body is grayish-white or cream-colored with a lighter spot on the chest.

The teeth of this animal are very small, except for the canines, which are considerably larger. Only the females have scent glands, which are located near the urogenitary tract.

Active and agile during the night, this civet is mainly a tree-dweller. It prefers thick forests but is known to have invaded coconut plantations. It feeds on vegetation and small vertebrates, especially rodents. The aban-doned nests of the giant squirrel apparently provide its shelter. The female gives birth to two or three young several times a year.

The Binturong (*Arctictis binturong*) is perhaps the best known of all the true palm civets. It is found in southeast Asia, Java, Sumatra, Borneo and Palawan. At first glance the binturong does not remind us of the other viverrids in the general appearance of its body, although its anatomical characteristics definitely place it within this family. It is a large animal, measuring as long as 6 feet. Heavily built, it may weigh from 20 to 30 pounds. Its body is covered with long, coarse hair which is longer on the tail than elsewhere. The coat is black, often touched with gray or fawn. The ears and sideburns have white edges that stand out clearly against this dark background. The ears are covered by long tufts of hair that drop downwards.

Strangely enough, the binturong has a monkeylike prehensile tail, an adaptation unknown in the other viverrid families. Also,

The small-toothed palm civet (below) has a very long tail, longer than its body. It lives in the thickest forests and has great tree-climbing ability, moving among the branches with ease.

Three mongooses of Madagascar: (top) the striped Madagascar mongoose, which owes its name to the five broad stripes on its light gray background; (center) the ring-tailed Madagascar mongoose; (bottom) the brown-tailed Madagascar mongoose.

unlike other civets, it walks ponderously, rather like a bear, planting its whole foot on the ground.

Not much is known of its habits, but we do know that it prefers night to day and lives in trees. At night, when it walks it moves slowly, using its tail as a fifth leg. Its daytime habits are equally cautious.

Apparently it prefers fruits and vegetables but has been known to eat meat.

Generally these civets mutter and make hissing sounds which turn into loud grumbles when they are annoyed.

Asiatic Palm Civets and Malagasy Civets

This subfamily is usually divided into four groups—the Malagasy civets, the true hemigales, the "otter" civets and the small-toothed mongooses.

The Malagasy Civet (*Fossa fossa*), the only species of its kind, inhabits Madagascar. It must not be confused with another viverrid species, the fossa (*Cryptoprocta ferox*) which is also a native of Madagascar.

This species has no anal glands, and the legs seem to be especially well built for running. The animal is about 2 feet long and has a gray coat with a reddish cast and four rows of black spots along its sides that are often fused together into horizontal stripes. It eats both flesh and fruit—it is especially fond of bananas—and in dry regions eats insects and lizards. Its habits are nocturnal, and little else is known about it.

The Banded Palm Civet (*Hemigalus darbyanus*), found in the Malay Peninsula, Sumatra and Borneo in southeastern Asia, is nearly 3 feet long and weighs about 4 pounds. It has a very bright, white-orange coat, with black spots arranged transversely along the back, on the tip of the tail and on the face. Near the neck there is a crest of hairs grow-

ing toward the front. The five toes on the paws have strong, curved, retractile claws.

The scent glands are small. There is not much information about its habits, except that it feeds on worms and ants, and the female probably gives birth to one young at a time.

The Borean Mongoose (*Diplogale hosei*), known only on the island of Borneo, is about 3 feet long. It is omnivorous and arboreal.

Owston's Palm Civet (*Chrotagale owstoni*) is a very rare species. About 4 feet in length, it is found in Laos and Vietnam. The coat is much like that of the striped palm civet, except for small black spots on the sides of the neck and the body. The secretion of the anal glands is particularly repellent.

The falanouc (skull and picture above) has such obscure relationships with the mongoose that for a long time it was classified as an insectivore. Note the long pointed head and small, conical teeth.

As its name suggests the otter civet (left) has aquatic habits like those of the otter. Its toes are partially webbed, and its teeth bear a resemblance to those of the pinnipeds.

45

The "Otter" Civet (*Cynogale bennetti*) resembles an otter in appearance and, like the otter, is fond of the water. It is a native of the Indonesian islands of Borneo and Sumatra. Measuring almost 3 feet long and weighing about 9 pounds, it has a short-haired, light-chestnut coat and long, thick whiskers. The toes are joined together by small membranes which aid in swimming. The animal emits a faint-smelling substance from an area near the genitals. Equipped with long, sharp premolars—important for seizing and carrying prey—and high flat molars used for chewing, this civet feeds on fish, crustaceans, mollusks, birds and small mammals. It can also eat vegetation. Although it spends much time in the water, it is a relatively slow swimmer but a very good climber.

The Small-toothed Mongooses of the genus *Eupleres* consist of two species: *E. goudotti* and *E. major*. Both live on the island of Madagascar. As adults, the two forms are distinguished by their different sizes. The former is generally less than 3 feet long and the latter more than 3 feet. The coat is chestnut in males, grayish in females. In both, the tail is covered with long, bristly

The suricate, a south African viverrid, lives a social life and has markedly daytime habits. It is, in short, rather different from most of its family. In addition, it becomes domesticated with relative ease and is sociable with man. Its resting position is characteristic: it sits on its hind paws.

hairs. These animals have pointed noses and short, conical teeth, reminiscent of those of the insectivores. Their paws are large with long, nonretractile claws. They hunt during the night for insects, larvae, frogs, lizards, mammals and small birds. They have no scent glands or anal sacs. Both species are rather docile and affectionate with people.

Galiidines—the Malagasy Mongooses

Four genera are distinguished in this subfamily, having a total of eight species.

Known by the general name of Malagasy mongooses, these viverrids are found exclusively on Madagascar. In all representatives the first toes are somewhat raised above the ground, the claws are not retractile, and the female has a double uterus but only one pair of teats. They somewhat resemble the true mongooses and the viverrines.

Malagasy mongooses are always slender and elegant looking. They all have long tails covered with hair that is considerably longer on the underside and at the tip. The natives like to keep them around their homes to eat rodents and cockroaches.

The Madagascar Ring-tailed Mongoose (*Galidia elegans*) grows to a maximum length of 2 feet, about half of which is tail. It has a dark-chestnut coat and its tail has chestnut rings. The throat is white. Only the female has scent glands. This mongoose feeds on insects, lizards, small birds and very small mammals. In its general appearance it resembles a squirrel.

The Madagascar Broad-striped Mongooses of the genus *Galidictis* comprise two species, *G. striata* and *G. fasciata*. Both are about 2 feet long and have gray or light-chestnut hair with broad black bands on the back. Only the females have scent glands. *G. striata* usually has five black bands on the back, whereas *G. fasciata* has from eight to ten bands.

The Narrow-banded Madagascar Mongooses (*Mungotictis lineatus* and *M. substriatus*) have never been studied in detail. The coat in both species has narrow parallel horizontal bands.

The Brown-tailed Madagascar Mongooses are two species of the genus *Salanoia*—*S. uni-*

The African, or common mongoose (top left) is the only one of its kind whose habitat includes part of Europe.

The marsh mongoose (top right) is large for a mongoose, with a stubby face and bristly fur. It hunts small, aquatic animals in the swampy zones in which it lives.

color and *S. olivacea.* Not more than 18 inches long, the former is reddish in color with black spots, while the latter is olive-brown with yellow spots. Again, little of their habits is known.

Herpestines—Suricates and True Mongooses

The true mongooses belong to this subfamily. They are small viverrids, with long, non-retractile claws and well developed anal glands. Their coats are never spotted and only rarely do we see some individuals with transverse stripes. The feet may have four or five toes, and the soles of the paws are generally hairless. The tail tapers like a brush, differing from those of the genets. Found primarily in Africa, they are active during the daytime.

The groups that make up this subfamily are (1) the suricates and (2) the mongooses.

The Suricate (*Suricata suricata*), also called **Meerkat,** is a typically south African form, with four toes on each foot. It measures about 2 feet, including the tail, and is covered with gray fur; the head is of a lighter color and there are yellowish tints on the tail, which has a black tip. Suricates have 36 or 38 teeth. They eat roots, insects, larvae, snakes, eggs, lizards, birds and small mammals. They prefer to circulate in the daytime and enjoy taking sun baths. They live in colonies and are very sociable, communicating through a variety of calls and murmurs. They howl when frightened and can also bark. The female gives birth to two or four young.

The True, or Common, Mongooses belong to the genus *Herpestes.* There are about eight species distributed throughout southwestern Europe, southern Asia Minor, Africa, Arabia, India and the Sunda Islands.

Europe's only mongoose, *Herpestes ichneumon,* belongs to this genus. At its largest it attains a length of 3½ feet and a weight

Several species of the common mongoose have elongated noses and bristly fur, making them resemble hedgehogs. Two are illustrated here (above left and below right) from western Africa.

The banded mongoose (opposite) is an African species of smaller size.

of 6½ pounds. The coat varies from yellowish-gray to chestnut-brown and some individuals are a combination of white and brown.

These mongooses have long tails and sharp snouts, five toes on each foot with sharp, curved claws, 40 teeth and scent glands near the anus. The various species live in areas covered with thick vegetation, as well as in dry open terrain. They are active during the daytime, hunting for food in groups of four to twelve. They feed on snakes, small mammals, frogs, fish, crustaceans, insects and birds.

The Indian mongoose has earned the reputation of a snake killer, especially of the cobras. One such encounter is immortalized in Rudyard Kipling's "Rikki-Tikki-Tavi." Highly agile and endowed with quick reflexes, it can seize the snake and crack its skull before the cobra is able to bite it and inject its venom. The female gives birth to two to four young after a 60-day pregnancy.

The African Dwarf Mongoose (*Helogale parvula*) is the smallest of the mongooses. It has no burrow of its own but travels in gypsy groups of up to a dozen individuals. It hunts in daylight, living on spiders, insects, snails and lizards, many of which it finds in abandoned termite mounds, where it also takes shelter. Small as it is, it combats snakes. Measuring about 15 inches long, it has a grayish-chestnut coat, darker about the legs, 36 teeth, paws with five toes and three pairs of teats.

The African Tropical Savannah Mongoose (*Dologale dybowskii*) inhabits the plains of

The dwarf mongooses are sociable in their habits and go snake hunting in groups. Pictured opposite is a typically African species.

the Sudan, Uganda and Congo. It is about 2 feet long, with a tail measuring from 6 to 9 inches. It has a grayish-white coat that shades to chestnut in the legs. Little is known about the habits of this species.

The West African Water Mongoose (*Atilax paludinosus*) is an animal with short claws and hairless pads. It is about 3 feet long, with a very dense chestnut coat sprinkled with black. It lives mainly in swampy areas and around the estuaries of rivers, though its toes have no traces of webbing. It hunts by the water's edge, preying on the animals that have taken refuge among the rocks along the shore. It also ventures into the water, diving in search of food. When attacked, it is capable of totally immersing itself in water, with only its nose tip showing. Its diet also includes birds, small mammals, frogs, crabs, snakes, insects and eggs found in the dry areas. Oddly, for an aquatic ani-

mal, it has no web between the toes, perhaps because it feels about in the mud for its prey.

The Striped Mongoose (*Mungos Mungo*) is distributed in tropical Africa. It is a small animal with a chestnut-gray coat and yellowish or white transverse bands running down its back. About 2½ feet long, it is usually found near streams (similar to the West African water mongoose). Its paws have five toes, the paw pads are hairless, and the claws of the forefeet are unusually large. The female has three pairs of teats.

This mongoose is gregarious, and like other members of its tribe roves in groups of six to 20 individuals, a community that is most active during the morning and evening hours, when it rummages through brush and grass in search of insects, rats, eggs, small reptiles and wild berries and other fruits. While searching for food, the animals chatter; when alarmed, they bark.

The white-tailed mongoose, an African viverrid, lives in the wooded areas of Eritrea and Somalia. It hunts small vertebrates during the evening hours and is a valuable destroyer of poisonous snakes, insects and harmful rodents.

The yellow mongoose, the only species of the genus Cynictis, lives in colonies of up to 50 individuals. It drives other animals from their den, often killing them in order to take over their homes. The species is typical of South Africa. Its fur is yellow-orange, whence its name.

The Cusimanses, genus *Crossarchus*, has three species native to the west-central zone of the African continent. These mongooses seem to prefer living in forest areas. Measuring about 2 feet long and weighing about 3 pounds, they have long claws and a coat that is spotted with chestnut, gray and yellow. The soles of the feet are hairless. They travel in groups of from ten to 24 individuals, wandering in search of reptiles, crabs, fruit and insects. They are very talkative, grunting,

chattering or twittering to each other. Not very much is known of their breeding habits. They are primarily daytime creatures; their life span is approximately six years.

Kuhn's Viverrid (*Liberiictis kuhni*) is the only species of a new genus created for eight skulls from the northeastern forest of Liberia that were sent to Germany after their discovery. This species has four upper and lower molars on each side, instead of the

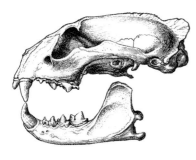

three found in the genus *Crossarchus*, which it otherwise resembles in skull features. Almost nothing is known about these animals, which have never yet been captured alive, except that they are said to be black, to live in groups of from three to five individuals, and generally take shelter in hollows of trees.

The White-tailed Mongoose (*Ichneumia albicaudia*) has 40 teeth, in contrast to the three preceding genera, which have 36 teeth. The paws have five toes and the soles are hairy. The coat has an overall grayish appearance, and two-thirds of the end of the tail are white. It measures over 3 feet long. Unlike many other mongooses, it is a solitary animal, rarely even forming couples. It hunts both in the afternoon and at night, eating much the same food as other viverrids—reptiles, insects, termites and small rodents. In the morning it hides in earthen burrows or abandoned dens. Although the female has four teats, she seems to give birth to only two young at a time. This mongoose occupies a wide territory ranging from Ghana to Nigeria and from the Sudan to Somalia, occupying both southern Africa and southern Arabia.

The Black-legged Mongooses of the genus *Bdeogale* comprise three species from eastern

(above) The skull of the Madagascar fossa has an almost feline look. It is rather rounded, with a short nose and a strong mandible.

(right) The principal carnivore of Madagascar is the fossa, a large member of the viverrid family, similar to a feline because of its retractile claws and its dentition. It is a ferocious animal about which the natives of Madagascar have woven numerous legends.

Africa, but one from the west coast is also known. They are all slightly over 3 feet long and show great variations in coat colors, with black legs predominating. These forms are distinguished by having four toes rather than five. Little is known about their habits, except that they probably bear one young at a time. They have hairless soles on the front paws, hairy soles on the hind feet.

Meller's Mongoose (*Rhynchogale melleri*) is distributed in Africa from Tanzania and Rhodesia in the north to Nyassa and Mozambique in the south. All four paws of this animal are covered with hair. Measuring about 3 feet in length, it is pale chestnut-gray in color with darker-colored legs. It is a retiring animal, most active during the night. Its food is mainly wild fruits and termites. The female gives birth to two young at a time.

The Yellow Mongoose (*Cynictis penicillata*) lives in southern Africa in the arid zones of brush near rivers and in rocky terrains. Measuring about 2 feet, it has a yellow-orange-brown coat that changes colors with the seasons and a white-tipped tail. There are five toes on the front paws and four on the hind ones. It lives in large colonies composed of up to 50 members. Sometimes they use dens abandoned by other animals for shelter but this situation rarely lasts. They prefer to dig their own complex system of tunnels which serve to link up a large number of bigger burrows. They seem attached to their shelters and do not wander far from them. This mongoose is mostly active during the day, except in densely populated areas. As with other viverrids, its diet consists of small animals, birds, birds' eggs, reptiles, termites and insects. Its habits are neat, and special areas in the colony are used to leave their excrements. The female gives birth to two to four young.

Selous' Mongoose (*Paracynictis selousi*), is distributed throughout southern Africa. It is about 3 feet long, with gray fur and a white-tipped tail. It has four toes on each foot, with long, slightly curved claws. The

Most fossas are reddish brown, but occasionally a solid-black one appears. Although referred to as fossa cats, they walk flat-footed like bears rather than on their toes as cats do.

secretion from the anal gland has a very strong odor. Primarily nocturnal in its habits, it is timid and retiring. Like the yellow mongoose, Selous' mongoose also digs complex underground chambers, but although burrows adjoin, this species does not appear to be colonial.

The Fossa (*Cryptoprocta ferox*) is not to be confused with the fanaloka, or Malagasy civet (*Fossa fossa*). It is the sole representative of this subfamily. Found only in Madagascar, it is the largest carnivore on the island. It measures about twice the size of a house cat—about 5 feet from nose to tail and about 15 inches high at the shoulder. It looks rather like a large oriental palm

civet. Its teeth, 32 in all, resemble those of the cat family and until recently it was mistakenly classed in the felines. It has short legs and walks in plantigrade style. Its claws are sharp and retractile. Its pale brown fur is short and dense and its whiskers are long.

Fossas are numerous and feared by the natives for their attacks on their henhouses. Birds and lemurs are their preferred food, but they are known to prey on pigs and calves as well. Nighttime hunters, they sleep in trees by day. Generally they avoid man and each other, but they may gather in groups of four to eight in mating season. The female gives birth to two or three young at a time. In zoos, their average life span is 17 years.

The Hyaenidae—The Sanitary Engineers

It seems probable that the hyenas made their first appearance in Asia. Recent excavations have brought to light fossil hyena remains from Asian Miocene deposits.

The living forms of this family are divided into two subfamilies, the Hyaeninae, or true hyenas, characterized by powerful jaws and teeth adapted to cracking very large bones and by four toes on each foot, and the mild, meek Protelinae, or aardwolves, with only three upper premolars and a weak dentition.

The Spotted Hyena (*Crocuta crocuta*) ranges throughout most of Africa south of the Sahara. Superficially, it resembles a dog but it actually is related to civets and mongooses. It

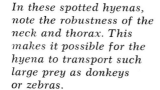

In these spotted hyenas, note the robustness of the neck and thorax. This makes it possible for the hyena to transport such large prey as donkeys or zebras.

55

has the characteristic shape common to the hyaenid family—a broad face, round ears and sloping hindquarters. The forelegs are markedly longer than the hind legs and contribute to a clumsy walk. Its coat looks moth-eaten, being yellowish gray with round, chestnut-to-black spots. The lower jaws are especially strong, probably the most developed in proportion to its size of any other mammal. These jaws enable it to play the role of a kind of garbage collector, for hyenas earn their living by cracking and crushing the bones of carcasses, thus clearing the plains of carrion. They can easily break the bones of such large animals as buffaloes and oxen.

Generally cowardly, they will attack, if driven by hunger, anything from sheep up to old lions and even small rhinoceroses. Because of their strong neck muscles, they can drag off prey as big as a donkey.

Known as the "laughing hyena," this animal has one of the strangest cries in the world, a sound like a sharp laugh. Another demonic sound starts deep and low and rises to eerie, penetrating heights.

Another peculiarity is the fact that both male and female have similar external sex organs, leading to the belief that they change their sex. It can reproduce at any time during the year. The period of gestation is about 110 days, after which the female gives birth to twin jet-black pups that take a long time to wean.

Solitary creatures, they prefer to range about at night. Several of them will gather about a carcass to quarrel over the remains and utter their weird cries. Their travels can be easily traced, thanks to the dung droppings made white with lime by their diet of bones.

The Striped Hyena and the **Brown Hyena** constitute the two members of the genus *Hyaena*. The former (*Hyaena hyaena*) lives in India, North Africa, Kenya, western Pakistan, Afghanistan, the Transcaucasus, the southern part of Russian Turkestan and Asia. The brown hyena (*H. brunnea*) can be found in southern Africa, reaching as far as Rhodesia and Mozambique.

Besides their separate areas of distribution, these two species are distinguished by the different arrangement of the stripes on a grayish background in the region of the neck and legs; the brown hyena has a grayish head and stripes on the parts of the body distant from the paws.

Both these species have a crest of long, erectile hairs in the neck region that con-

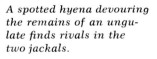

A spotted hyena devouring the remains of an ungulate finds rivals in the two jackals.

tinues down the length of the back. They are of smaller size and have longer ears than the spotted hyena. The total length rarely exceeds 4 feet, and the weight varies between 60 and 120 pounds.

For shelter, these animals prefer rock crevices or holes in the ground. Like the spotted hyena, they are nocturnal, but they are not aggressive. Only if they are threatened do the striped hyenas react with a low grumble, erecting the crest on their neck and spine. They feed mainly on carrion. The brown hyena frequently appears along beaches, seeking refuse thrown up on the beach for emergency food.

Both the striped and the brown hyena have large glandular sacs beneath the tail that hide the external sex organs and make it difficult to determine the animal's sex. After three months gestation, the female gives birth to from two to six young.

The hyena has an unsavory reputation which in many respects it does not deserve. In exploiting its particular niche in the natural scheme of things—that of a garbageman —it is as useful as any other animal of the jungle or desert. Although it is known as a carrion eater, for example, most of its food is actually bones, for by the time the hyena

Striped and rather long fur, long pointed ears, a generally slender shape, and an elongated nose characterize the striped hyena (above). It can be distinguished at first sight from the stocky spotted hyena.

(left) Hyenas do not like intense heat, and when the sun is overhead it is common to see them, like this spotted hyena, cooling off in the water.

57

reaches the remains of a kill, vultures have usually stripped the carcass of all flesh. The hyena, therefore, is left to finish off the skeleton, which it does with great efficiency, often leaving nothing behind. Its feces is very characteristic: being composed mainly of bone fragments, it hardens to a rocklike consistency which, found in fossil form in Europe, provides irrefutable evidence that extinct forms of the hyena once wandered far north of where they are found today.

Protelines—the Aardwolves

The Aardwolf (*Proteles cristatus*), is the sole representative of this subfamily. It is distributed in eastern and southern Africa. Ranging from 2½ to 3 feet in length, the aardwolf is smaller than the striped hyena, which it resembles. It has a soft, wavy fur of a yellow-gray color with black stripes that extend down to the first joint of the legs. From the nape of the neck, a thick crest of bristly long hairs runs down the length of the back. When it is threatened or frightened, it erects this crest, which gives it a quite formidable appearance.

It is frequently found in the open plains or in brushland, where it inhabits either the abandoned burrows of other animals or digs burrows of its own. The aardwolf feeds on termites, insect larvae, beetles, small rodents and birds, and only rarely on scraps left over from the kills of larger animals. It does defend itself when cornered, using its sharp canines and emitting an unpleasant odor of musk from its anal glands. Generally, these animals live solitary lives, but occasionally they may gather in groups of five or six.

During the day they take shelter in burrows. The female gives birth to from two to four young. Certain of the females of this species raise their young communally.

Hyena cubs (opposite) show how difficult it is to distinguish the cub of the striped hyena from one of the spotted variety.

(below) The only species of its kind, the aardwolf has an erectile crest of long thick hairs on its back. It is similar to the striped hyena, with which it is easily confused despite its smaller size. The aardwolf feeds mainly on insects, although it will eat carrion on occasion. Its teeth are widely spaced and not very strong.

The brown hyena (left) is very similar to the striped hyena in its conformation, but its coat is of uniform color.

59

The Felids—The Great Hunters

The felids fall into two subfamilies—the saber-tooths, now all extinct, and the felines. Both groups appeared near the beginning of the Oligocene, some 35 million years ago, with the felines continuing successfully into the present. There are 36 species in this family, including the domestic cat.

Living Felines

Their movements are silent and they hunt by careful stalking, followed by a sudden rush on the quarry. Their most characteristic features are the teeth and claws.

The teeth are admirably designed for stabbing, biting and slicing. Powerful neck and jaw muscles enable them to seize and immobilize their prey by breaking its backbone. The claws are retractile, with an action that turns the foot into a formidable weapon. At the same time that the claws are unsheathed, the toes spread out, making the foot twice as broad as it normally is. The forelegs have five toes, and the hind ones have four.

The powerfully muscled legs are capable of great leaps and spurts of speeds—the cheetah can attain 70 miles per hour. At the same time, the animal is so well coordinated that it always lands on its feet when it falls or is dropped. If need be, it can swim for great distances.

The teeth are typically carnivorous, totalling 30 in all. The mandible has six incisors, two canines, six premolars and two reduced molars (some felines have four molars). The carnassial teeth are highly specialized, and the canines are particularly well developed.

The tail may be long or short; the fur is soft and thick. Sometimes the animal is uni-

Although life is now very difficult for the big cats, tigers can still be found in fairly large numbers in the jungles of India and southern China, and in other isolated jungle areas of Asia. Tigers are the largest members of the family Felidae and hunt such game as leopards, crocodiles, and even other tigers.

This skull below belongs to the king of beasts—the lion. Note the roundness of the head and the short, strong jaws. The canines are sharp and the carnassials well developed.

(above) Diagram of the claws of the felines, with the ligaments that make possible retraction and extension.

form in color; sometimes there are spots or stripes. Hearing and sight are very well developed in the felines. The pupil of the eye may, when contracted, look like a narrow slit. In length, these animals range from a foot or so to 12 feet including the tail.

The gestation period in felines lasts from 60 to 100 days (60 days for the domestic cat, 100 days for the lion and the tiger). The cubs, which number from two to six, are carefully brought up by the parents, with whom they live for more than a year. Because they are around their parents so much, they learn hunting techniques and self-protection methods from them. In hunting felines either act individually, like the cat or the leopard, or they adopt group strategy, like the lions.

The felines are found in Eurasia, Africa and the Americas; they are not distributed in the Australian regions, the Celebes, Madagascar, Iceland, Polynesia, the Antilles or in the extreme arctic and antarctic latitudes. Characteristic genera and species are found in the different regions. For example, the puma and the jaguar are found in the Americas; the lion is an established inhabitant of Africa and Asia; the tiger is found in India, China, Thailand, Sumatra and Java.

Until a short time ago all the felines were considered as belonging to the single genus, *Felis*, with the only exception being the cheetah, assigned to the genus *Acinonyx*. Today the genera *Neofelis*, *Uncia* and *Leo* have been added.

The genus *Felis* includes animals of small and medium size. The puma, the ocelot, the domestic cat and many others are in this grouping. This genus has 29 more species, more than any other genus in the family Felidae.

The genus *Neofelis* has a single species, the clouded leopard, *Neofelis nebulosa*, of southeast Asia, which is characterized by very large canines. The genus *Leo* is comprised of all the large cats—the lion, the tiger, the leopard and the jaguar. The snow leopard is assigned to a separate genus, *Uncia*, and so is the cheetah, which, as already noted above, belongs to *Acinonyx*.

A lion in the grassland drags along its prey. Unlike other felines, the lion does not stalk its victim for a long time before bringing it down, but lies in wait and attacks by surprise. If the victim flees, the lion does not follow it.

Cats of the Genus Felis

The European Wildcat (*Felis silvestris*) lives in the forests of Europe and Asia Minor. The fierce wildcat bears a strong resemblance to the domestic cat. It can be distinguished, however, by its larger size, markings of black stripes rather than blotches, and the black tip of a tail that is rounded rather than pointed. Wildcats also have larger heads and teeth than domestic cats, although, surprisingly, their intestines are shorter. Both wildcats and domestic cats are about the same size, about 4 feet long, including the tail.

The European wildcat has gray coloring, verging on a reddish, yellowish, or blackish hue, with black markings. It is an excellent climber and can travel from one part of the woods to another along the branches of trees, easily surprising birds in their nests.

When on the ground, wildcats usually hunt alone or in pairs, each animal keeping to an area of about 150 acres, and marking off that territory by leaving claw marks on

All the members of the felids are recognizable "cats" with distinct family resemblances. The house cat (left) and the cheetah at left below are obviously related and in many ways share the same living habits.

The illustration below shows clearly the difference between the three "classical" spotted furs of the felines: the leopard (top), the ocelot (center), and the jaguar (bottom). In the first we note the characteristic rosettes formed of groups of five or six spots; in the second, the spots are oval and elongated; in the last, the circles are polygonal with smaller spots in the center and a strip of solid spots in the middle of the back.

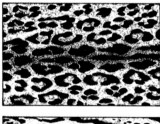

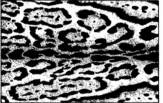

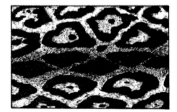

63

The European wildcat, though rare, is found in many isolated areas of Europe and Asia Minor. Although it resembles a large domestic cat, it belongs to another species.

trees that serve as boundary markers. They hunt small mammals and birds, and apparently even attack small deer and fish. Nocturnal in habits, they stalk their prey.

Mating takes place in the spring, and after a period of 63 days the kittens (usually from four to six) are born in a den. The females care for their young for about six months; the male takes no part in their raising. Occasionally a male wildcat has been known to breed with a female domestic cat.

The African Wildcat (*Felis lybica*) is also known as the Libyan or tawny wildcat. It bears close resemblance to both the European wildcat and domestic cats. Common in north and central Africa, it is also found in some regions of Asia and on the islands of Sardinia and Majorca.

It is a little larger than the domestic cat, measuring about 30 inches long, including 10 inches of tail, and weighing about 9 pounds. In appearance, this cat is much like the European wildcat, except that the stripes on its body are not so distinct and the undersides sometimes have a tinge of yellow.

The African wildcat has nocturnal habits, feeding on small mammals and birds and sometimes even reptiles. This cat will breed freely with the domestic cat if given the opportunity.

The Jungle Cat (*Felis chaus*) is about 30 inches long and weighs about 20 pounds. It can be found in Egypt, the Middle East, Asia Minor, Russia, India and Ceylon. It is gray-brown in color, with lightly striped markings; the tail has deep-black rings. It eats birds up to the size of a peacock, as well as small mammals.

This animal has a definite resemblance to the lynx—short tail, long paws and small tufts of hair on the ears. Although it is most active at night, it is not exclusively nocturnal and can be seen during the daytime among thick bushes or tall grasses. It climbs very well, and birds are its main food, although it does eat small mammals. The females have between three and five kittens in the spring.

The Leopard Cat (*Felis bengalensis*) lives in tropical Asia, Java, Sumatra, Borneo and the Philippines. Measuring about 32 inches long, it has soft, thick fur, which is reddish in color, turning to white near the stomach. The fur is covered with round spots or with stripes.

The leopard cat lives in hilly areas, where it is a good climber. Its prey consists of large birds and small mammals. Usually the litter includes three or four young.

The Lynxes are now all placed into the genus *Felis*, although at one time they were assigned their own genus, *Lynx*. They are medium-sized, smaller than leopards and larger than wildcats. They have long legs, large paws, short tails and tufted ears. They have two upper molars as against three for typical cats. Their head is short and broad and they have impressive side whiskers. The fur is generally long and soft, light brown or gray with darker markings.

There are three types, the northern lynx, which lives in North America; a Eurasian species, which is found in central Europe and Asia; and the bobcat. Lynxes generally feed on small mammals and large birds. They live in forested areas, spending most of their time in the branches of trees.

The Common or Northern Lynx (*Felis lynx*) was once, along with the wildcat, the most numerous feline of the European primeval forest. Now it is exceedingly rare, probably because it tends to flee man. A few still hold out in Spain, Portugal, Sardinia, and parts of the Balkans. Sizable numbers are found only in the U.S.S.R.

This lynx is very well built and can move quickly over short distances. It is an expert climber, often hiding on tree branches. It feeds on small mammals and ground-dwell-

Similar in appearance to a lynx, the jungle cat (lower left) prefers the swampy banks of rivers.

The leopard cat (lower right) lives in the forests of tropical Asia. It is an agile tree-climber and is always on the hunt for birds.

ing birds, never eating carrion and rarely attacking man.

Mating occurs between January and March, and after a gestation period of 70 days the female gives birth to from two to four cubs.

The European lynx has been successfully tamed, and during the 19th century was used for hunting, much like the cheetah.

The Leopard Lynx (*Felis lynx pardellus*), which is even rarer, is found in southern Europe, particularly in Spain. A little more than 3 feet long, it is distinguished from the northern lynx by its darker coloring, the greater length of its side hairs and its smaller size. It was hunted almost to extinction because of its beautiful fur and tasty flesh.

The Pallas cat (below), a felid of the central Asian steppes, shows an aggressive mood.

The caracal (a lynx) is an intelligent animal; it wears out its prey before capturing it. At one time in Asia, the caracal (lower right) was trained for hunting small-sized game.

The Canadian Lynx (*Felis lynx canadensis*), also called the arctic lynx, inhabits the Canadian forests from Labrador to Alaska, but it is also found in the northern United States as far south as the 38th parallel. It feeds primarily on hares, which it can catch easily because of its speed. The thick fur on its paws act like a snowshoe. When hares are scarce during the winter months, the Canadian lynx will attack foxes, fawns, birds and other mammals. It is an able tree-climber.

The females give birth to one to four cubs after a 70-day pregnancy period. The lynx cubs are born blind and remain so for several weeks. Their fur is striped and spotted, unlike their parents' fur, which is long, thick, soft and predominantly cream-gray in color with light-brown spots. In the adult the tip of the tail is black and the eyes are encircled with white. The Canadian lynx is a timid animal and avoids man completely.

The Red Lynx (*Felis rufa*) or bobcat ranges the forests from southern Canada to southern Mexico. It was once probably very numerous in the east coast forests. They are still numerous but very careful to avoid man, and they seldom venture out in daylight. They prefer heavy vegetation for protective coloration and travel generally along the branches of trees.

Smaller than the Canadian lynx, the bobcat has almost tuftless ears. Its black markings are distributed in a different way, and its color varies between red and olive-brown. The belly is white with small spots. The tail has black rings and a black tip.

When cornered, it is ferocious, spitting, screaming and hissing in a terrifying manner. It has been known to overcome a coyote even when caught in a trap.

The mother has two to four young which live with her for six months.

The Caracal Lynx (*Felis caracal*), also called the desert, or Persian, lynx, can be found in large numbers in southeastern Asia and Africa. Its color is uniformly reddish-brown on the back, white on the undersides, with two white marks over each eye. The exceptionally long ears end in tufts of hair. Measuring about 2½ feet long, caracals are notably proficient jumpers and runners and are active both day and night. They live in grassland and brush and feed on fawns, gazelles, rabbits, pheasants, grouse and other animals of medium size. They can be domesticated and trained to hunt. The female usually has two or three young in an underground den or hollow tree.

The Manul Cat or Pallas's Cat (*Felis manul*) owes its name to a man named Pallas who discovered the species in 1778. It can be found in rocky areas in the steppes of central

The common lynx (left) is unmistakable in appearance; the characteristic "sideburns" are clearly visible in this photograph.

The Canadian lynx (below) is similar to the common lynx; it is only slightly smaller in size. Its fur is long and thick.

The margay (right) of South American forests, no bigger than a domestic cat, is gaining favor as a household pet.

Asia, from Tibet to Siberia and from Afghanistan to China. It feeds on rodents, partridges and reptiles.

The coat is basically orange-brown, and there are white and black rings around the eyes. The forehead is gray with black spots and the chin is white. The hair is very long and soft. In overall appearance, this cat has a flat-headed look because the eyes are positioned high in the forehead and the ears are low. These characteristics enable the animal to remain well hidden behind rocks while readying an attack on its prey.

The Serval (*Felis serval*), or African leopard, inhabits the bush country of Africa below the Sahara. It is never found in very dry regions or very far from water. It is most commonly found in central Africa, where it hunts fran-

The serval (bottom left) is distributed throughout Africa but is more common in the central regions of the continent. Because of its daring raids into villages, where it slaughters every kind of small domestic animal, the native population hunts the serval with every means it possesses.

Temminck's cat (bottom right) is a large wildcat that inhabits the southern regions of Asia and the island of Sumatra. Its fur has a uniform golden-brown color that is unusual among the wildcats.

Though it normally feeds on small mammals, this fishing cat will also eat fish, which it catches with a quick sweep of its paw when the fish are swimming along the surface of the water.

colins, small birds, guinea hens and small antelope.

The average size of the serval is about five and a half feet, including the tail, which is short. It weighs about 34 pounds. Its head is relatively small, and it has fairly large ears, long slender legs and thick paws. Characteristic of this animal are the longitudinal rows that form a regular pattern on the cat's body and the broken rings on the paws and the tail.

After a gestation period of about 70 days, the female usually gives birth to three young.

The Marbled Cat (*Felis marmorata*) inhabits southeast Asia, the Malay Peninsula, Java, Sumatra and Borneo, where it shows a preference for wooded areas. Its name comes from the pattern of its fur—blackish stripes and spots resembling the veining of marble on a yellowish background.

A nocturnal animal, measuring about 3 feet in length, of which half is tail, it feeds on small mammals and birds. It is said to be capable of domestication.

Now very rare, this cat hunts on the ground, in clearings and along river banks.

Temminck's Golden Cat (*Felis temmincki*) is a large wildcat about 3 feet long. It inhabits the slopes of the Himalayas in Nepal and Assam, China, Malaysia and Sumatra.

This animal has a characteristic rare among cats—a uniform golden-brown color. The muzzle, however, is a mixture of white, gray and black. A rare animal, it lives in rocky areas and hunts rodents, fawns and birds. Generally the female gives birth to two young in the hollow of a tree.

The African Golden Cat (*Felis aurata*) from western Africa is a species very similar in appearance to Temminck's cat, except that it is somewhat smaller. It lives in deciduous forests near the coast, from Sierra Leone to the Congo.

The Fishing Cat (*Felis viverrina*) is usually found near water in the swampy forests of the Indochinese region, Java, Sumatra, Ceylon, India and Malaya. It feeds on small mammals, birds and fish, which it catches with a lightning slash of its webbed paw. It is said to be a ferocious and aggressive animal.

The fishing cat is heavily built and short-legged. It measures about 32 inches in length and weighs about 17 pounds. Its gray coat, spotted black, is of a harsh texture when compared with other members of the cat family.

The Ocelot (*Felis pardalis*) is famed for its beautiful fur, which is made into luxurious fur coats. A native of the Americas, the ocelot ranges from southwestern Arkansas, Texas and Arizona southward to Paraguay.

This animal lives in forests and areas of thick vegetation, hunting only at night when near human settlements, but otherwise active both day and night.

The fur is short and smooth, its color ranging from a grayish to a yellowish hue—the grayish tones being preferred by furriers. The animal is marked by gray-black oval shapes with black borders that stand out sharply, creating a beautiful design down the back. The belly and paws are white.

The head with its flattened profile and pronounced ridge on the back of its skull strongly resembles that of the large felines of the genus *Leo*. The adult male sometimes reaches a length of 4½ feet, including 15 inches of tail. The female is slightly smaller.

The ocelot can climb trees with great agility, and it spends most of the day sleeping on a branch. Much of its hunting is done on the ground, where it prefers small animals such as opossums, rodents such as the agouti, small deer and reptiles. It is not considered dangerous to man, from whom it flees in terror.

Not much is known about its reproductive habits, except that the female gives birth to a pair of cubs sometime between September and January. Today the ocelot is protected, with hunting being limited by laws and regulations, because the animal is in danger of becoming extinct.

The Tiger Cat (*Felis tigrina*) of Central and South America can be found from Honduras to Paraguay. In South America it is found only east of the Andes. This cat, too, is sought for its fur.

The tiger cat strongly resembles the ocelot, but it is slightly smaller, measuring about

70

3 feet in length, with a 15-inch tail. The tiger cat's oval spots, bordered by a black band, are larger than those of the ocelot; the tail is longer and the head is rounder.

This animal lives in groups in the trees, and overlaps the ocelot in distribution. It hunts birds and small mammals and is known to make raids on domestic animals.

The Margay (*Felis wiedii*) resembles the ocelot. About the size of a large house cat, it hunts animals in a neotropical forest.

The Mountain Cat (*Felis jacobita*) is also known as the Andean cat. This species is only found in South America, living in the mountains of Chile, Argentina, Peru and Bolivia. Its fur is brownish-gray with darker markings on the sides and rings on the tail. It measures 30 inches in length and feeds on rodents.

Geoffroy's Cat (*Felis geoffroyi*) is named after a 19th-century French naturalist who discovered the species. Its range is from Bolivia to southern Argentina. Resembling the mountain cat, this cat, however, is usually found lower down, in the foothills. It hunts birds and small mammals, often plunging onto its prey from overhanging branches.

The Kodkod (*Felis guigna*) lives in the foothills of the Andes Mountains in southern Chile. It is a small animal, measuring approximately 18 inches in length. The fur is

The young jaguarundi (opposite page, left) and the Geoffrey cat (opposite page, right) are typical of the species found in Central and South America.

The young puma (left), with its characteristically marked coat, must be five or six months old before its fur takes on the uniform tawny coloring of its parents.

These little spotted cats (left) are natives of South America, where they live in forested or brushy areas.

a grayish-brown with rows of darker spots; the tail has black rings. It lives in woodlands, hunting small mammals and rodents and sometimes even raiding henhouses.

The Jaguarundi (*Felis yagouaroundi*) or otter cat has a large territory ranging from southern Texas to Central and South America.

Measuring about 4 feet, its body is long and graceful with short legs. Its weight is about 20 pounds. The ears and nose seem small for a cat. The color of the fur is a uniform reddish-brown or gray. These two colors led some zoologists to believe there are two species, but they came to the conclusion that this cat goes through two distinct color phases. Generally speaking, it looks more like a large weasel than a cat.

A good climber, it prefers to live in thick, dry underbrush through which it can slip quickly. Visible in the daytime, it prefers to range at night, when it hunts small birds and mammals, frogs and fish. The female generally has two to three young, which are born with light spots.

The Pampas Cat (*Felis colocola*) is another cat that is in danger of becoming extinct. It is about the size of a domestic cat and has a relatively long tail. Its range is from Chile to Argentina, as far as Patagonia. The fur is gray, and the markings are brown.

Along the back runs a crest of longer hair. It hunts at night for small birds, rodents and other mammals. The female gives birth to from one to three kittens.

The Puma (*Felis concolor*) is also known as the cougar and the mountain lion. It is the largest member of the genus *Felis* and one of the two largest American cats. It is the most widely distributed cat in the Americas, extending from British Columbia in the north to Tierra del Fuego in the south. It can be found in pine woods, tropical forests, prairies and deserts. Because of this widespread distribution, different local races are recognized. The largest can reach a length of 8 feet, and its weight can range from 80 to 260 pounds.

The head is small compared to the body. The fur is sand-colored, shading to off-white. The ears and part of the muzzle are black, and the tail tip is dark.

The puma is a great hunter, its favorite prey being medium-sized hoofed mammals, such as deer. It will tackle almost any animal that comes within its range, however. It is one of the few animals able to kill a porcupine by turning the animal on its back and attacking its soft, defenseless belly. The puma usually has a litter of two or three kittens.

The Clouded Leopard (*Neofelis nebulosa*) inhabits southeast Asia, Sumatra, Java and Borneo. It is a great climber and seems to prefer to remain unseen, hiding in the thickest jungles on branches of trees.

The head and body measure about 3 feet, and the tail adds another 30 inches. The body is graceful and slender, weighing about 45 pounds, which is light for so big an animal.

These animals are night-hunters, preying on birds and small mammals. They have also been known to attack sheep, pigs, goats and even dogs.

The body is covered with thick, soft fur, light gray or brown in color. The markings are large spots with a black border that is ringed in white. Nothing is known of its breeding habits in the wild. In zoos, litters of from one to four cubs have been born.

The canine teeth of this feline are proportionately considerably longer than those of

This clouded leopard is an Asiatic feline of limited distribution. Characteristic of this species is the length of the canines, which, in relation to its size, are among the longest among present-day felines.

the other cats, and it is therefore not placed in the genus *Felis* but in a separate genus, *Neofelis*. There are also other dental and cranial features that make the clouded leopard distinctive.

In Borneo, the canine teeth are used by certain natives as ear ornaments, and seating mats are made from the skin. The Chinese for centuries have used dried parts of the body for medicinal purposes.

In captivity, the clouded leopard is gentle and playful and likes to be petted by its keepers. Several zoos in the United States have been successful at breeding them.

The Big Cats

The Genus Panthera includes the four big cats of the feline family. These are all prized by the hunter, and their numbers are diminishing. Three of them, the lion, the tiger and the leopard, live in the Old World, while the jaguar lives in the New World. All four cats have retractile claws, and all have a supple-suspensory ligament of the tongue bone permitting them to utter impressive sounds.

A group of lions feeds in harmony on the carcass of an antelope.

The Lion (*Panthera leo*) is the second largest of the cats. Commonly called the "king of the jungle," it lived within historic times in southern Europe and roamed the Middle East as well as India and Africa. But man has driven this majestic beast from all but a very small part of its old area. Symbol of the sun, it was considered fit game for royalty and in India a single sportsman might kill 300 lions. Today, only about 200 exist in Asia, all in the game preserve of Gir Forest in India. The lion is relatively common only in east-central Africa.

Not all lions look alike. There is quite a variety in appearance and in breeds. In general the males, by the time they are five years old, have a mane of specialized long hairs on their heads, shoulders, chest and elbows, but the distribution varies from lion to lion as does the color. The color of the fur is yellowish gray, much like the color of dried grass, with a black tuft on the tip of the tail.

Male lions measure from 6½ up to 9 feet and weigh about 400 pounds. A lion is said to be in his prime between 4 and 10 years of his age. Some zoo lions have been known to live 25 years, but this is rare in captivity and probably impossible in the wild, where 15 years is considered to be a ripe old age.

A noisy animal, the lion makes good use of its modified larynx to frighten animals. The sounds range from a slight moan to a mighty roar. He uses both teeth and claws to make a kill, but sometimes a mere swat of his paw will down an animal the size of an antelope.

The lion has 30 teeth but uses its four canines to hold the prey, kill it and tear the meat. Four carnassials cut through tough skin and tendons. Lacking flat teeth for chewing, he has to swallow his food in large chunks.

Once a kill has been made, lions proceed to dine on the spoils in a very systematic way. First the blood is licked up, then the favorite parts are attacked—the kidneys, liver, thigh muscles and ribs. One large meal can satisfy a lion for a week, since he is capable of consuming about 50 pounds of meat at a sitting.

Lions are most active at night. They hunt in efficient but loosely organized packs. The female hides in the grass while the male stalks its prey upwind. At the crucial moment, when the quarry catches its scent, the male roars and leaps, taking care to drive the terrified victim into the waiting claws of the female.

Charging, the male can reach the speed of 35 miles per hour. Lions will defend their prey but rarely fight over a kill among themselves. They kill only what they need.

A lioness has interrupted her meal for a moment. Although lions normally feed on animals that they themselves have killed, they do not reject the carcasses of animals that have been left behind by hunters.

75

Lions hunt a great variety of prey and have been known to kill rats and mice. They eat carrion if other preferred game such as zebras, gnu and antelopes is lacking. Giraffes and young elephants are also high on the list of favored foods.

In zones where man has settled, lions will attack domestic animals and even man himself. Lions who have had a taste of human flesh lose their fear of man. They will even initiate their cubs to this taste and after that the pack can well become a menace to an entire region. Essentially, however, the lion is not a man-eater.

Lions live in a large social group called a pride, composed of one family or several. Life within the pride is generally peaceful, especially as lions sleep about 20 hours a day. Lionesses are usually three or four years old when they bear their first litter. There is no particular mating season, for lions can breed at any time of the year. The gestation period lasts about 108 days, after which the mother gives birth to two or three cubs. As lions do not have permanent dens, the mother must move the cubs from one place to another by carrying them in her mouth one at a time.

A lioness is shown suckling her young. After three months the young lions generally begin to eat meat.

presence they are now accustomed. The lion is also rather easy to keep in captivity, and they quite readily reproduce in zoos and circuses. If the lion cannot really be domesticated, it can be trained, as everyone realizes from watching circus performances.

Lion training is one of those incredible feats that must be seen to be believed. The precise scientific basis on which it is done is a matter of argument. Most likely, what is involved is a distortion of ordinary social behavior. Animals that live in groups naturally have a relationship with others of their kind. They may, as a result of fighting or of

(left) A lioness followed by her cubs drags off the remains of a large buffalo.

Lions are primarily animals of Africa's great plains, but they have also taken to rocky highlands, escaping from the huge inroads which man has made on their habitual territory.

The cubs are weaned at eight weeks, when they are led by their mother to a recent kill to share in the spoils. After that, their education is a good example of how young carnivores learn hunting techniques. First the cubs observe their parents hunting and share in the spoils. When they are ten months old, if their teeth are well developed, they begin to hunt on their own while their parents stand by to help if necessary. The cubs remain dependent on the pride until they are two years old and thoroughly capable of capturing their own game. Lionesses usually wait until their first litter is independent before having a second litter.

Having already become extinct in most of the areas where it once was king, the lion is now on the road to extinction throughout all of Africa. For example, the magnificent Cape lion with its unusual black mane became extinct as long ago as 1860.

Aside from the hunter's gun and the trapper's cage, the major menace to the lion is the disappearance of the large herds of herbivorous animals that it needs for food.

In order to prevent the complete extinction of this magnificent animal, measures have been taken to protect it. In the national parks of southern and eastern Africa, lions are frequently observed on the roads, unconcerned by the cars and visitors, to whose

Though not truly arboreal, lions are at home in trees, as this happily slothful group amply demonstrates.

bluff, be of high "caste," lording it over their fellows, or they may be subordinate in position. When in contact with members of other species, a social animal sooner or later starts to treat these as if they were members of its own kind. A lion tamer, then, becomes accepted by a group of lions as another "lion." He does this gradually from outside the cage, and he must learn to read the mood of each animal from the signals it makes. He must impress on each one that he is the superior and dominant animal. When the time comes for him to step into the cage, there must be no doubt. The trainer must establish his position by bluff, for in actual physical combat he would certainly have no chance at all.

The Tiger (*Panthera tigris*), like the lion, has long been the prey of man. In India it was hunted by princes, wealthy sportsmen and professional hunters. The price of a tiger hunt is royally high—$2,000 to $2,500. Larger than the lion and the largest feline in Asia, the tiger is both feared and revered in India by man.

But lion and tiger used to live side by side. Now the lion lives on a reserve while the tiger's domain extends from central Asia, northeast China, parts of Iran, India and Burma southward to the Malay Peninsula, the Indonesian islands of Java, Sumatra and Bali. "Shere Khan," as Kipling called the tiger, is about 4,000 strong in India.

They are dangerous when stalking prey and when a tigress is disturbed with her cubs they are not by nature man-eaters despite their fearsome reputation. Perhaps two or three in a thousand become eaters of human flesh—doubtless the old and feeble individuals who are unable to pursue faster prey or females who are raising their young in areas where wild game is scarce.

To nourish themselves tigers will attack almost any animal, including large elephants and lions. Although they live in forests, they are not particularly good tree climbers. They hunt mainly at night and generally alone. They attack large prey in a terrifying silent rush, but they prefer to pounce on small prey. After the kill, they hide the spoils, returning to the carcass again and again.

Like the lion they have useful and powerful vocal chords which can start with a short bark, a cough or a hiss and end in a great roar.

Indian male tigers measure 9 feet or more from nose to tail tip and weigh 400 pounds. Their relatives in Manchuria and Siberia are even larger. The Siberian is the largest living feline, weighing 550 pounds.

The fur of the tiger is red-gold, with clear black stripes and black markings on the forehead. The pattern of the body striping on one side of the tiger varies from that on the other.

Lions are social animals and live in small groups, like the one shown above, called "prides." During the mating season, however, a male and female will leave the pride and spend some time in solitary intimacy.

Groups of lions like these are rarely seen during the day, even in those areas where they are common, for their color blends well with the landscape.

79

In general those living in the northern regions are paler than those of south, a difference attributed to their need to camouflage themselves in various environments. White tigers with ice-blue eyes and dark brown stripes have been reported, but they are very rare.

immerse themselves in water, a preference that sets them apart from other cats. Tigresses give birth to four or five cubs after a pregnancy of about four months. Generally, only two cubs of the litter survive. The young are born with woolly striped fur, and they remain with their mother until they are two

The base coloring of the tiger is reddish yellow, darker on the back, lighter on the sides and whitish on the underside. Transverse stripes cover the whole body from the tail to the head. The stripings on the head have a characteristic pattern.

The tiger has a sinuous elegant action that hides its force, for it can bring down a buffalo with a quick spring of its powerful body. Its sense of hearing is very acute, but its senses of smell and sight are less so. Curiously enough, although these animals have lived in tropical regions for a very long time, they suffer from the heat and like to

years old and have learned how to hunt alone.

If lion and tiger mate, the cubs are called ligers if the father is a lion and tigons if the father is a tiger. However, such cross-breeding is not successful because the male offspring is often sterile and unable to reproduce its own cubs.

The Leopard (*Leo pardus*) is the smartest of the cats, although it is smaller and less fierce than the tiger. While it is perhaps one of the most dangerous of jungle animals, it has been able to adapt to encroaching civilization better than the lion, for it can live both in the tropical rain forest and in the drier langur monkey. Other wild prey include deer, antelope, wart-hogs, impala, waterbucks, baboons, large rodents, birds and domestic dogs, a variety of food that guarantees that the leopard never goes hungry in the forest.

But whether it is hunting wild game or

This Siberian tiger is a representative of the largest living feline. Because of its vast range of distribution, the tiger has adapted to very different habitats. The commonest environment, however, is the shady, steaming jungle.

open country of southeast Asia. It is there, in close contact with the domestic animals of the farms, that it prefers to stalk its prey, rather than hunting the monkeys, deer and piglets of the forest. But the leopards inhabiting the forest are agile tree-climbers, and a favorite food for Indian leopards is the tame farm animals, the technique is the same. It hunts at dusk, by sight or by smell, both senses being acutely developed. Leopards are silent and efficient stalkers; they kill either by breaking the victim's neck or by severing the jugular vein with the teeth. It prefers to hunt alone.

The leopard is the most widely distributed large feline in Africa and Asia. It has a yellowish-brown coat thickly covered with black spots in the form of rosettes. Besides its coat, another characteristic of this feline is its cylindrical tail, uniformly covered with hair to the tip.

Having made its kill, it then establishes a larder much like the dog that buries a half-finished bone for a later meal. First the leopard licks up the blood, then it eats the entrails before dragging off the rest of the carcass to a hiding place. Sometimes it even pulls the remains up into a tree, where it lodges them in a forked branch far from such hungry scavengers as jackals and hyenas.

During the Ice Age leopards were found from the British Isles to Japan and southern Asia. Now they are extinct in Europe and Japan but plentiful in Africa, southern India, Ceylon and Java.

Because of the market value of the leopard fur, the animal is actively hunted or trapped at night when it goes after domestic animals that have been set up as bait.

In general its coat is pale ochre, deepening sometimes to a reddish hue spotted with black rosettes. Some leopards are black and are called black panthers. Variations on the basic theme include the gray Persian leopard, the reddish-brown Java leopard, the African leopard with its more concentrated spots and the larger Chinese leopard, which has longer hair.

A good-sized leopard will measure 4½ feet long plus an additional 3-foot tail. It weighs about 100 pounds, although animals weighing 200 pounds have been known. Small and lighter than either the tiger or the lion, it is gracefully proportioned.

Leopards will breed at any time of the year. Two to four cubs are born at the end of a three months gestation period, but it is rare that the whole litter survives into maturity.

Leopards (left and below) are beautiful and agile animals. The design of the spots on the coat offers distinction for each individual, for they vary in shape and position. No two leopard skins are identical.

The Jaguar (*Leo onca*) is not only the biggest cat in the New World, it is also the only large spotted feline to be found in the northern, central and southern parts of the Americas.

It bears a strong if superficial resemblance to the African and Asian leopard. In Mexico, where it is still to be found, it is known as *el tigre*.

It is about the same size as the leopard, measuring an average of 7 feet including the tail. However, the shape is quite different. The leopard is graceful, but the jaguar is almost clumsy-looking, with its large head, heavy body and ponderous stomach. It has a short tail in comparison to its length and walks with a curious rolling gait.

The fur is yellowish in color, with markings of deep black rosettes. Toward the tip

of the tail, the markings become circles. Where leopards have rosettes bearing no center spot, jaguars have several small additional spots within each rosette. There are rare cases of pure black jaguars which, as among the leopards, are a result of hereditary factors and can crop up in any litter of normally spotted cats.

Jaguars are found inhabiting thick forested areas. They are particularly good climbers, often feeding on birds. They are also very good swimmers, sometimes catching and killing turtles and alligators. Jaguars utilize the same hunting methods as do the other big cats; they stalk their prey and then make a leaping, short-range, surprise attack. They kill a wide range of animals for food, including large rodents, deer, tapirs and even fish.

In the spring, after a gestation period of about 100 days, the female gives birth to from two to four cubs. These cubs are more heavily marked than the adults, bearing random spots that later form rosettes. They reach maturity in about the same time as the other big cats—two years.

The jaguar rarely attacks man, and it seems to be less feared than the other large felines.

The Snow Leopard (*Uncia uncia*) belies its name, for it is neither a typical leopard nor does it live in regions of year-round snow.

It roves the mountain ranges of Russia, Siberia, Mongolia and western China, especially the Altai and Sayan ranges. Adapted to the thin, cold air of such regions, it never goes below 6,000 feet in summer and generally lives at altitudes between 10,000 and 20,000 feet. It migrates with the seasons and can always be found at the snow line in winter.

Other cats do not have a specific breeding season, but the snow leopard does, possibly because of the rigorous living conditions. Mating occurs in late winter, followed by a gestation period of about 100 days. This permits the cubs to be born in April just as the weather becomes warmer. There are generally two to four cubs which live with their mother in a den for two months. The cubs are then permitted to go on hunting trips with their mother. They continue to live with her for about a year until they become accomplished hunters.

The total length of the snow leopard is somewhat more than 7 feet, including the 3-foot tail. It is thought to weigh about the same as the African leopard. Compared to the leopard, the snow leopard appears to have a smaller head and a longer body with smaller legs. Often it is thought that the snow leopard is bigger than it actually is because its fur is unusually thick.

The fur of the snow leopard is yellowish-gray in color, often with white undersides.

The jaguar is very similar to the leopard, and like the leopard it exhibits a great variability in its coloring. Lacking prey a certain size, jaguars will make do with any kind of animal, including fish, which they catch easily.

In the winter, the coat is much denser and slightly grayer in tone. The markings consist of large, black rosettes, having an indefinite outline. The tail has dark markings and looks extremely long because the hair on the tail is at least 2 inches in length. The back of the ears are dark at the base and much lighter at the tip.

Snow leopards are usually night hunters. They are capable of killing mountain goats, gazelles, deer, wild boar, birds, rabbits and ground squirrels.

As far as we know, snow leopards will not attack man, but this is hard to prove because of the remote areas in which they live. In fact it is difficult to ascertain not only their habits but also their numbers because of their preference for hunting by night and the remoteness of their territory.

Unfortunately their skins are highly valued in the fur trade, and many are trapped for this reason. They are caught in pits made wider at the bottom than at the top and baited with young sheep. Some are also captured in iron traps, and many of the animals offered to zoos have been maimed.

The Cheetah (*Acinonyx jubatus*) is definitely unique among all the big cats, not really resembling any of them in any concrete way. For that reason, it has been placed in a separate genus. Readily noticeable are the cheetah's superficial similarities to dogs. Among these are the length of the neck and the paws, the inability to retract its claws, its running ability and its method of hunting. However, the cheetah's ancestors are the same as those of other large cats, and

Both jaguars (a family group of which is shown to the left) and leopards occasionally come up with "melanistic" (solidly black) individuals. These can occur in any litter of normally spotted felines. The head below belongs to a black panther, as the melanistic leopard is called.

The snow leopard (bottom) lives in the Tibetan mountains at very high altitudes. The heavy fur helps it to withstand the freezing temperatures. It has larger spots and longer, thicker fur than the common leopard.

85

The big cats, like all the Felidae, (see leopard at right) are distinguished by their round head, a total of 30 teeth, and feet suited to tiptoe walking. Except for the cheetah (below) all species have claws that can be sheathed and unsheathed at will.

All the big cats have evolved some sort of camouflage in the coloring and pattern of their fur appropriate to the habitat. Thus the solid, tawny color of the lion (left) blends well with the savannah surroundings, while the stripes and spots of tigers (lower left) and leopards (lower right) fit equally well with the dappled jungle floor that is their home. Young lions show a fairly obvious spotting that fades later.

The cheetah lives in the equatorial regions between the two tropics. It prefers open grasslands, where it can better pursue its prey. Its general appearance suggests the greyhound, especially because of the length of the neck and legs. Its dense pattern of small spots makes for effective camouflage.

therefore there is no doubt among zoologists that the cheetah is a member of the cat family.

The overall length of the cheetah is about 7 feet, including the 2½-foot tail. It can measure up to 3 feet at the shoulder, but for its size it is quite light, usually weighing from 100 to 150 pounds. The head of the cheetah is small and round, and the jaws are weaker than those of the leopard or the jaguar. However, in general appearance the shape of the head, the length of the tail, and the markings on the fur are very much like those of the leopard.

The fur of the cheetah is yellowish in color, marked with solid black spots, not rosettes, that are distributed equally and densely over the whole body. The tail has rings, the short ears are dark with light tips,

and two dark lines run from the forehead across the eyes and down the sides of the face to the mouth. On the nape of the neck, in both sexes, there is a small mane, from which this animal got the name *jubatus*, meaning crested.

The cheetah can be found in Africa, from the Cape of Good Hope to Egypt. In Asia it is now found only in Iran, southern Russia and Afghanistan. Wherever it lives, it frequents grasslands. Formerly the cheetah had the same range as the lion, but hunting has severely reduced its number and distribution.

When hunting, the cheetah does not attack like the other big cats. It uses a very cautious approach to its prey. It slithers on its belly, as close as it can get to its victim, and then quickly leaps upon it. If the prey happens to get away, the cheetah chases after it at speeds up to 70 miles an hour—the highest speed of any mammal—and very few of the pursued ever win the race.

Unlike many of the other big cats, cheetahs do their hunting during the day, chiefly early morning and early evening to avoid the heat. Their favorite foods include gazelle, blackbuck, hare and guinea hen.

In India, cheetahs were even taught to hunt—a remarkable achievement considering the independence of spirit and savage ways of wild cats such as these. For although cheetahs, if caught young, respond better than most felids to captivity, their natural aggressiveness must be preserved intact if they are to serve as hunters for man. For this reason, only mature animals could be used, and these were trained in much the same manner as dogs or falcons. They were taken to the hunt with hoods over their eyes and released only when the game was near. Once let loose, they pursued the prey just as their wild brethren would. Because they cannot run at high speed for long distances, cheetahs can be caught easily enough by men on horseback, and this is insurance enough against their escaping once they made the kill.

The gestation period of the cheetah is about three months. The cubs, born blind, are able to retract their claws for about ten weeks. They are born with a long gray mane. This is soon lost, but the hair on the nape of the neck remains for life.

The skull of the cheetah is short and strong, typically feline. The dental structure, too, is characteristic of the felines, although the canine teeth are stubbier, like those of the Canidae.

The cheetah is sometimes referred to as a "hunting leopard," but is not included in the same genus as the leopards and other big cats. Cheetahs differ in that their claws are not retractable and the pupil of the eye is round rather than slit-shaped.

The Domestic Cat

A discussion of the family Felidae and the genus *Felis* would be incomplete without taking a look at the domestic cat, *Felis catus*.

Cats have a beauty and a silent strength that is missing in all other domestic animals. Their independence and aloof air is much appreciated by their admirers.

There is only one species to which all domestic cats belong; however, there are variations, called breeds, within that single species. Usually the breeds are divided into two main groupings, the longhairs and the shorthairs.

History and Distribution

Many believe that the cat was first domesticated by the Egyptians before 1600 B.C. Cats were used by the Egyptians to catch the rats and mice that were invading the grain storehouses. Because they did such a

A kitten of the short-haired domestic breed. The young are nursed until about the 35th day, after which they are weaned. They gradually adapt to the carnivorous diet typical of the species.

A shorthaired cat with tiger markings is shown on the opposite page. The term "tiger" is used for obvious reasons.

good job in destroying these rodents, cats were worshiped as gods. The Egyptians believed that the goddess Bast, who represented the life-giving heat of the sun, had the head of a cat. It is said that when a pet cat died, its Egyptian owner shaved off his eyebrows in mourning. The Egyptians so much revered the cat that they made dead cats into mummies and buried them in cat cemeteries.

The first cats were probably brought into Europe by Phoenician traders about 900 B.C. Cats brought from Europe to America in the 1700's by explorers, traders, and settlers are the ancestors of our cats today.

Legend and Folktales

There is a great accumulation of tales and legends about cats that have been handed down through the centuries. One legend has it that when Noah took all the animals aboard the ark in pairs, he did not have any cats because they did not as yet exist. The ark soon became overrun with rats and mice, so Noah asked the lion, the king of the beasts, for help. The lion sneezed and from his nostrils came two cats, which immediately destroyed most of the mice and rats. The remaining vermin were so afraid of being killed that they hid in holes and have stayed that way ever since.

Chinese legend says that the domestic cat is a cross between a lion, which provided it with its dignity, and a monkey, which gave it its curiosity and playfulness.

According to Italian legend, when Mary gave birth to Jesus, a mother cat, housed in the same manger, gave birth to kittens at the very same time. Italian artists have been influenced by this story and have often painted this scene. Cats are present in paintings by da Vinci, Floris, Durer, Bassano, Reynolds, Gainsborough and Renoir, to name but a few.

Japanese sailors believe that cats having the combined colors of red, white and black

are able to predict the coming of a storm. Therefore, cats are always to be found on Japanese ships.

There is a legend in China and Japan that, when Buddha died, all the animals gathered around his body and wept in sorrow. Only the cat and snake did not weep. Seeing a rat, the cat leaped upon it and killed it against the orders of Buddha. For this reason, cats are traditionally excluded from the zodiac.

Russian folklore says that the cat Ivanovitch, smart enough to marry a fox, reigned over all the animals in the forest.

A Polish legend tells us that when a litter of kittens was thrown into a river to drown, the willows nearby, hearing the sobs of the mother cat, agreed to join all their branches together so that the kittens could cling to them. Ever since the willows in the springtime have gentle buds that feel like velvet, much like the fur of a kitten, and in every country where they appear they are called by some name like our "pussywillows."

In the Brittany region of France, there is a story that in the fur of every black cat there is one white hair. If a person can find it and tear it out without being scratched, that hair will become a good-luck charm, making its owner rich or lucky in love.

Perhaps the best known folktale involving cats comes from Great Britain. Dick Whittington, a poor orphan, had a cat as his only pos-

A single-colored short-haired cat has been distracted by the photographer from its carnivorous meal. The ears of the cat can sense 20,000 to 25,000 vibrations per second, which is well within the supersonic range.

session. This cat, sent on a journey on one of the ships of Whittington's master, brought back a fortune to Dick, who then married his master's daughter and became lord mayor of London. Similar legends in which a cat brings its master a fortune are found in the folklore of Denmark, Italy and Iran.

In the Ozark mountains of Arkansas, when a woman receives a marriage proposal and she cannot decide whether to accept or refuse, she takes three hairs from a cat's tail, wraps them in white paper and puts them on her doorstep. The next morning she unwraps the paper, and if the hairs look like the letter y, she answers yes, but if they form the letter n, she answers no.

thought to be a good omen when a black cat crosses one's path. Some believe that it is lucky to own a black cat, but unlucky to meet one, or that good luck will come to anyone who strokes the animal three times. Other beliefs that are taken seriously by some are that a cat born in May is bad luck; if a cat leaves a home where a person is ill, that person will surely die; if a cat sneezes near a bride on her wedding day, the marriage will be a happy one; if a cat sneezes three times in a row, members of the family will all have colds before long. It is also a fact that some fishermen's wives believe that their men will return safely if a cat is kept in the house.

The shorthaired domestic cat (left) in its many varieties (single-colored, tricolored, tiger, tabby, etc.) belongs to the group that also includes such cats as the Siamese, the Russian blue, the Chartreux, and the Abyssinian.

Two basic characteristics of the shorthaired cat (below) are the round head and the ears, broad at the base, pointed and located high on the head.

Throughout the years the cat has been associated with occult beliefs, especially with witchcraft. It was thought that witches sometimes took the shape of cats, and that cats owned by witches were their "familiars."

In the United States, the black cat is considered bad luck; in Great Britain, it is

As you can see, cats mean different things to different people, today as much as long ago. But to many, a cat is just a beautiful animal and a nice pet to have around. Because it has been a favorite pet of many for so many thousands of years, the domestic species has branched out into many breeds.

The Abyssinian cat, shown here in a variety of attitudes, is the one breed, of all modern forms, that most closely resembles the sacred cat of ancient Egypt.

General Characteristics and Anatomy

Perhaps the most obvious cat characteristic is its determined independence, even though it has been domesticated for several thousand years.

Cats possess their own language. When a cat purrs, it is content. Cats seem to meow only to people and not to other cats. In addition, they spit, hiss, growl and scream at various times. Their faces are particularly expressive, showing anger, pain, fright and pleasure. Ears pointed forward express happiness; ears flat against the head show that a cat is angry.

The similarities between domestic and wild cats do not involve outward appearance

Abyssinian cats have been very popular since their introduction into Western society in 1869 by an Englishwoman. They are unusually dependent upon human companionship and continue active at play long after kittendays.

only. They move in the same way, walking on their toes rather than on the whole foot, and they can move at great speeds. They are all excellent climbers, except for those whose size makes them clumsy.

The cat is a particularly cautious animal, but when faced with danger, it does not usually run away but stands its ground, arching its back to appear larger than it really is.

The cat's eyesight is its best developed sense. Since a cat in the wild does most of its hunting by night, its eyes are capable of increasing the amount of light passed through the retina. This is done by way of a reflecting layer that is located behind the retina and called the tapetum. The cat is better able to focus on moving objects than on stationary ones, and it is particularly good at judging

A shorthaired cat (right) sharpens its claws on a wooden pole. House cats rarely use their claws enough to counteract normal growth, and to keep them of proper length the cat should have a piece of wood on which to claw.

distances, an important trait for any animal that hunts for its food. Although the color of a cat's eyes can have many variations, cats seem to be color blind, seeing things only in different shades of gray.

The cat's body is very flexible, allowing it to be graceful, fast and effective in hunting down its prey. The strongest muscles are in the back, the hind legs, the neck and the shoulders. The vertebrae of the spinal column are connected by muscles rather than by ligaments, resulting in greater elasticity. The breastbone is elongated and the shoulder joint is very flexible, permitting the forelegs to move freely in many directions. All these adaptations make it a very agile animal.

It is interesting to watch a cat walk or run. Unlike other animals, such as a dog or a horse, the cat moves both the front and back legs on one side of the body at the same time, much in the manner of a giraffe. Most animals move the right front leg with the left hind leg and the left front leg with the right hind leg.

The claws of the cat are curved and very sharp, perfectly adapted for grasping prey. They are retractile, with the claws normally hidden and extended when needed. A cat can, and usually does, walk silently, with its claws retracted, so that it is able to make a surprise attack on its victims. Cats periodically scratch their claws against hard surfaces to remove the worn outer shells. They normally have five toes on their forefeet and four toes on their hind feet, but it is not rare for a cat to have six or seven toes. This is a hereditary abnormality.

During their lifetime, cats have two sets of teeth: 20 milk teeth shed at about six months of age, and 30 permanent teeth. The canines are very long and sharp, enabling the cat to stab and kill its prey.

The cat's tongue is long, flat and rough. This permits it to lick every piece of meat off a bone. The cat also uses the tongue to clean itself.

Here a shorthaired cat (right) with tiger markings lies lazily in the sun with half-closed eyes, obviously relaxed and content. Many animals enjoy the sun, and none more than the cat.

The cat's hearing is very sharp. It can hear high-pitched sounds that are way beyond the range of human ears. The shape of the external ear—the fact that it stands erect —also helps the cat to catch every sound.

The only places that fur does not cover the cat's body are the nose, the pads of the feet, the anus and the nipples. The coat is shed and regrown every spring and fall. The cat has whiskers on the eyebrows and face made up of coarse hairs called the *vibrissae*. Because they are very sensitive to touch the vibrissae serve to protect the face.

Female kittens five months old are capable of being mated. Cats do not have limited cycles as dogs do, and they may come into season every few weeks during spring and summer, each cycle lasting anywhere from a few days to about three weeks. If the female is not mated, it will come into season again almost at once. When a female is in season, it lets the males know by calling.

It is possible for each kitten in a litter to have a different father, as the female can conceive several times during one mating season. The average period of gestation is 62 days, after which time usually four or five kittens are born. Each kitten is born in a separate sac which the mother splits with her tongue, cleaning the kitten off at the same time. The mother will also eat the placenta. This action stimulates the milk.

Kittens should not be handled by people during the first two days or so after birth. They are born with their eyes closed, but they are very sensitive to light right away. The eyes remain closed for about ten days. Adult male cats, with the exception of Siamese, should be kept away from the newborn litter, as they are inclined to harm the kittens. The mother cat nurses the kittens for about two months.

This calico shorthaired cat watching its reflection in the mirror is almost certainly a female. The abnormally high proportion of females in this breed, long known to cat-lovers, can now be explained in the light of modern genetics.

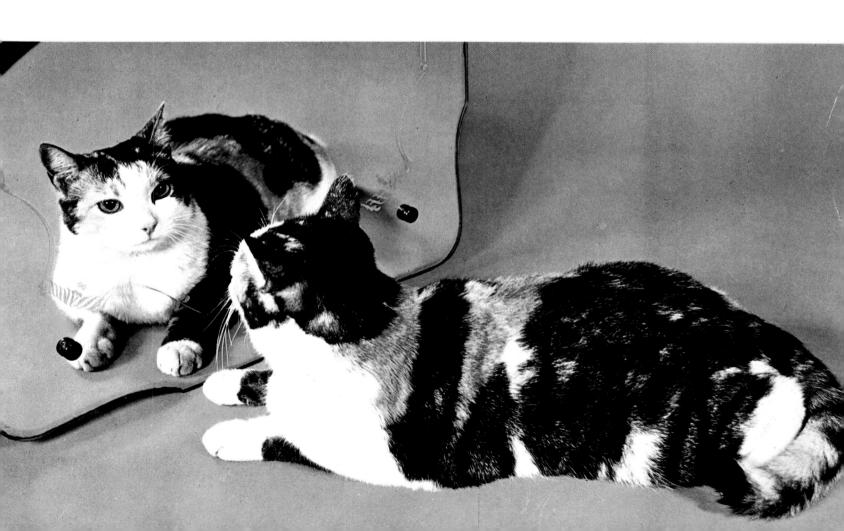

Siamese cats have been known to have as many as eight or nine kittens; Abyssinian cats usually have only one or two.

The Longhair Breeds

Longhaired cats are the result of cross-breeding Persian and Angora cats. Angoras originally came from Ankara, Turkey. Persians came from Iran and Afghanistan. Both types were first brought to the United States by traders from the Orient during the 16th century.

Persians come in many color varieties. In general, they have short bodies, round heads, snub noses, small ears and bushy tails. The hair is long and thick, and a particularly fluffy collar of hair encircles the neck.

The Black Persian is one of the oldest of the longhaired breeds. It should be free of any markings. To keep the coat pure black, a blue Persian should be bred with a black

This calico Persian with its young will not abandon the kittens after weaning but protect and train them until they are three or four months old. During this period, she teaches them to distinguish friend from foe.

98

from time to time. The eyes should be large, round and either copper or deep orange in color, without a trace of a green rim. The kittens are born with a very ugly color which usually does not improve for about six months. At birth, the coats can be gray or rusty, with white hairs running through. The body shape of the black should be short and thick, the same as for all Persians. The neck should be strong, the shoulders broad and flat, and the legs short.

Blue Persians are particularly appealing. Any shade of blue is acceptable, but the color must be constant throughout. There should be no white hairs, shadings or marks of any kind. The body and eyes should be like those of the black Persian. The female is generally smaller in size than the male.

Red Tabby Persians have a deep orange color marked by darker bands. The markings must be clearly defined, appearing on the body, chest, legs and tail. A common fault is a white tip on the end of the tail, and this is most difficult to breed out. The eyes should be deep orange or copper. Bad characteristics that are fairly common are large ears and narrow heads.

Red Persians are very difficult to breed, and a perfect red is very seldom seen. The color should be a deep, clear red, with the roots showing the same coloration as the tips. The biggest difficulty is in eliminating the tabby markings.

Cream Persians are becoming increasingly popular in the United States. Again, the color is what is most important. It has been said that this color of Persian originated from the mating of a blue and a red. The objective is a pale color overall, consistent in shade.

The Smoke Persian is a truly beautiful cat. Experience has shown that it is not advisable

to inbreed smoke to smoke for too many generations, as the markings will fade. The kittens are born either solid black or solid blue, with the white beginning to appear when they are about three weeks old. The most desirable color in a smoke Persian is an undercoat of white with the tips shading to black; the black should appear strongly on the head, back and feet. If this can be achieved, the result is one of the finest of breeds.

Research indicates that there are twelve hereditary genes involved in cat coloration. White coloring is related to a recessive gene and only appears when each parent has one such gene.

The head of the black Persian (top left) is round, broad, full-cheeked, with small ears which are spaced rather far apart.

The Chinchilla Persian (below) is a breed for which standards do not accept completely black individual hairs or markings.

This white Persian (right) shows green eyes which are often characteristic of the mature cats of the breed.

Tortoiseshell Persians are almost always females, as the color is sex-linked. These cats are a combination of red, cream and black. A tortoiseshell female is bred with a red,

cream or black male. Tortoiseshell males are always sterile. It is hard to breed a perfect tortoiseshell with a red that is dark enough or that carries patchings in equal distribution.

Calico Persians are very similar to the tortoiseshells, except that the former are marked with white as well as red, cream and black. This color is also sex-linked, and almost all calicos are females.

Blue-eyed White Persians are very difficult to breed because of the required eye color. Kittens born with blue eyes often have green eyes when they are grown. Deafness seems to accompany the blue eyes.

Copper-eyed White Persians are easier to breed than the blue-eyed ones. Also, they are not plagued by deafness.

Blue-cream Persians are very rare. The best color is obtained when a cream female is mated with a blue male. The male kittens will be cream and the females will be blue-cream. Blue-cream males are extremely rare and are always sterile. The two colors, ideally, should be evenly intermingled, with no patches of either color occurring. In the United States, however, patching is acceptable for show. A preferred specimen has a blue ground and cream patches.

Brown Tabby Persians are very difficult to breed with the correct markings. The ground color and the markings should be strongly

These two Burmese cats are splendid examples of a variety developed by crossbreeding Siamese with other stock. The Burmese is fairly well known in America, but it is practically unknown elsewhere in the world.

contrasted; the head should be barred between the ears and down the neck, continuing down the back and under the body, where it comes together in the middle of the stomach. The eyes should always be copper.

Silver Tabby Persians have a silver ground color. This should be pure, not marked with gray or rust. The markings should be black. The eyes should be green or hazel.

The Chinchillas and the shaded silvers are the only cats that should have black penciling around the eyes. The kittens are born with silver tabby markings which become diffused throughout the body as the kitten grows. The shaded silver has heavier black tipping than the chinchilla.

The Shell and Shaded Cameos are a result of crossing the silver Persian with either a red or a cream. The shaded cameo has heavier tipping than the shell. The undersides of both cats are white.

The Angoras have long bodies, long ears and long noses. Their heads are pointed, in contrast to the Persians, which have rounded heads. Their tails are bushy and, like the Persians, they have a ruff around the neck. The fur is long and silkier than in Persians.

The tailless Manx cat, a breed resulting from a mutation, is a curiosity of nature. In perfect individuals the lack of a tail must be complete, with a slight depression present where the tail normally would be.

The tortoise-shell Persian cat (opposite page) is a breed in which the coloring is sex-linked; most tortoise-shells are female.

Peke-faced Persians are recognized as a breed in the United States but not in Europe. The cat's head shape is very much like that of a Pekingese dog. The forehead should be high and bulge out over the short, indented nose. The nose should be completely obscured in profile by very full cheeks. The muzzle should be wrinkled with folds of skin evident under the eyes and on each side of the nose. The eyes should be very large and round. The coat color is usually a bright, deep, uniform red.

Maine Coon Cats are semilonghairs, with thick, coarse fur. The coat may either be solid or tabby-marked. The face is longer and more pointed than that of the Persian. These cats have long bushy tails that are often striped. The legs of the Maine coon cat are long and thick.

The French Burman Cats are considered the sacred cats of Burma. They have only recently been accepted as a breed in the United States and Great Britain and are still rare in these countries. The history of the French Burman cat is very interesting. The Burmese priests believed that the faithful returned to the earth after death in the bodies of these cats, which were therefore worshiped and treated like gods. In color, the French Burman cats bear a strong resemblance to the Siamese. Ideally, the animal is very long but low-legged. The paws are short but strong. The head is wide and rounded, with full cheeks. The fur is long, silky and golden in color; it is slightly curled on the belly. The eyes are a deep blue. The paws should be pure white, and the mask, points and tail should be seal-colored.

The Himalayan, recognized as a breed only as recently as 1958, was developed by crossing a Siamese with a Persian. The coats are longhaired and light in color, with dark markings. The eyes are always blue.

The blue Persian (right) is a show breed for which the standards require consistent coloring throughout, although any shade of blue is acceptable.

The red tabby Persian (below) is the most popular of all the long-haired tabbies.

The Shorthair Breeds

The Black Domestic Shorthair should have no other color traces in its coat and should have copper eyes (most black cats have green eyes). This breed has been achieved by crossing tabbies for many years. The kittens are born with faint stripes, which ideally should completely disappear with maturity.

Domestic Blue Shorthairs and Domestic White Shorthairs are variant breeds, the standards in eye color being the only difference. The whites must have eyes that are very deep blue, copper, golden-orange or odd-eyed (one blue, one copper). The blues have eyes that are copper, orange or yellow.

Domestic Cream and Blue-Cream Shorthairs are rarely seen. The cream should have no trace of white in the coat, and the blue-cream should have a patched, rather than a mingled, coat.

The Domestic Shorthaired Tortoiseshell has a color that is sex-linked. Almost all these cats are females. The few males that do exist are sterile. The color of the coat should be an equal balance of red and black (light and dark) with no white at all. A red blaze on the head is desirable. The eyes should always be copper.

The Domestic Shorthaired Calico should be red and black (light and dark), with the color distributed equally on a white background. The white must never predominate, and the eyes should be orange, copper or hazel.

The Manx Cat is very unusual as it is the only cat born without a tail. Manx cats should have short backs and high, round rumps. The hind legs are longer than the front ones, making this cat run with a hop like a rabbit's. However, they are known to be able to run faster and longer than any other breed of cat. Manx cats got their name from the Isle of Man, where they originated. They were first brought to the United States in the early 17th century.

Domestic Shorthaired Tabbies can be brown, silver or red. In all variations, the tail must

(upper left) The smoky Persian is a variety highly prized by cat fanciers for the beauty of its coat. The fur of this variety, like that of all Persians, is thick, long and very soft, with a rich collar.

The blue Persian (upper right) developed by intensive interbreeding, is certainly one of the most beautiful breeds. The most highly prized color today is pale blue; in the past the darker blues were more popular.

The calico Persian (left) This cat differs from the tortoise shell only in the presence of white patches among the colors.

be evenly ringed, and it is highly desirable for there to be rings on the chest. The eyes on the red and brown tabbies should be copper; on the silver, they should be green.

The Mackerel-striped Tabby is perhaps the most common household cat. They are often called "tiger cats." The markings should be very dark and in the form of narrow rings, as numerous as possible. The rings should run in a vertical direction from the spine toward the legs.

The Russian Blue is an unusual-looking cat. The color should be an even bright blue throughout, with silver-tipped guard hairs. The head is flat and long, the face is broad across the eyes. The fur is very dense. The ears are relatively large, and the tips are more pointed than rounded. It is a large cat, with a long, muscular body and long legs. The eyes are round and bright green. It is rarely seen in the United States, but it is a very popular breed in Great Britain.

The Abyssinian is a warm brown color with dark-brown or black tipping. The eyes are green, yellow or hazel. There should be no markings on the head, tail, face and chest.

It is a medium-sized cat with a long, tapering tail and small paws. The breed probably originated in Egypt, but it has been bred in Ethiopia (Abyssinia) for a very long time. These cats are not very common in the United States.

Siamese Cats have long, slender bodies and short, sleek-looking fur. They are less independent than the other breeds, preferring to be around people more than the other breeds do. They come from Thailand (Siam) and were first brought to the United States from England in 1895. They have since become very popular in this country. The seal-point Siamese is the most numerous and the most popular. The eyes should be a clear blue; any green tinge is considered a fault. The coat of a seal point should be cream, becoming a pale fawn on the back. Kittens are born with a lighter color. Variant breeds include the chocolate point, the blue point and the lilac point. The chocolate point is a lighter shade than the seal point. It resembles the color of milk chocolate, and the color appears on the ears, mask, legs, paws and tail. The blue point has blue markings on the ears, mask, legs, paws and tail. Another name for the lilac point in the United States

The Burmese (below left) is a breed which has gained great popularity, in part because of the lovely sheen of its coat and because of its gentle, affectionate temperament.

The French Burman cat (below right) is the sacred cat of Burma, long worshipped by the priests of Lao-Tsun.

is the frost point (its points are a grayish-pink). There is a red-point breed recognized in Great Britain but not in the United States, its points being reddish-gold.

The Burmese Cat was developed from a cat brought to the United States from Burma in about 1930. This cat was a female, and she was mated with a male Siamese. The process of selection and mating was a long one, but eventually the desired breed was created. In 1954, it was recognized as an individual breed by the Governing Council of Cat Fancy.

Ideally, the body of the Burmese cat should be much like that of the Siamese, that is, long and thin. The tail is long and pointed, again very much like the Siamese. The face, however, is all its own; it is wedged-shaped and shorter than that of the Siamese. The eyes must always be yellow; in the Burmese blue eyes are a disqualifying feature. The coat is a dark sable, shading slightly lighter on the stomach and chest. The kittens are born with points much like adult Siamese, but as they grow the points fade and the cat becomes uniform in color.

This cat seems to be as affectionate and as fond of people as the Siamese. It is also less excitable.

The Siamese seal-point kittens at the top when fully mature, will resemble, the adult shown at the lower right.

(lower left) The Burmese is a breed which was developed by mating a native Burmese female with a male Siamese. It was recognized as a separate breed in 1954.

107

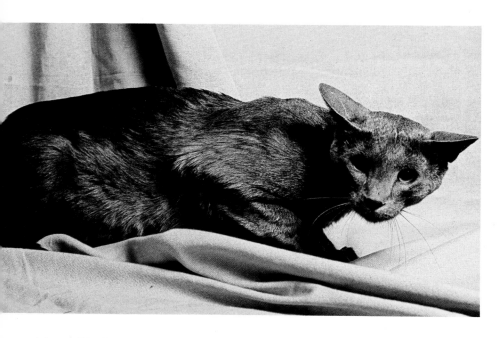

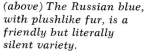

(above) The Russian blue, with plushlike fur, is a friendly but literally silent variety.

The black Persian (right) is one of the oldest of all longhaired breeds. To qualify for showing, the black Persian must be free of all markings.

The Havana Brown Cat was named for the tobacco color of its coat and not, as many think, because it came from Cuba.

The Havana brown actually originated in England and was bred by crossing a black shorthaired female with a chocolate-point Siamese male. The kittens of this first matched pair were then mated together to create the first Havana browns.

The breed is known to be very even-tempered. It is about the same size as the Burmese cat, but the fur is longer and the eyes are yellow-green in color.

The Rex Cats are one of the newest additions to the breeds of cats, first recognized as recently as 1959. On most cats the hair is straight, but on the rex cats each hair is wavy. The hair is shorter than in any of the other short-haired types mentioned.

When the rex cat is crossed with a cat of another breed, the wavy coat is always passed on to the young. Even the whiskers of the rex cats are wavy. The color of these cats can vary to the same extent as in the domestic shorthairs, which makes for some very interesting possibilities.

The Health of Cats

Normally, a healthy cat has a pink tongue and a cool, moist nose. If the tongue becomes coated or the nose is dry and warm, it may be a signal that the cat is sick.

The most serious disease a cat can get is distemper. Kittens that contract distemper invariably die. Symptoms are a high fever, inability to eat or drink although it may appear to want to, running nose, watery eyes, fits of sneezing, uncontrollable vomiting and diarrhea. There are actually several kinds of diseases that are called "distemper." Vaccination by a veterinarian when the kitten is about ten weeks old serves as a safeguard against the most dangerous kind.

Hair balls may form in a cat's stomach from the hairs it swallows when cleaning itself. A symptom of this condition is often a dry cough with no other indication of a cold. It may also vomit or have constipation. A mild laxative is often an effective way of ridding the cat of hair balls.

Cats are also susceptible to worms. Outward signs appear in the cat's coat; it may become dry and rough, and shed often. Some cats with worms refuse to eat; others want to eat all the time but they cannot put on any weight. The worms and worm eggs are excreted with the animal's other wastes, and a stool examination is needed for diagnosis. There are medical ways of freeing the cat from worms.

Fleas often get into a cat's fur, causing skin irritations. They are found mostly on the head, ears, neck, rump and tail. Both the cat and its sleeping quarters should be treated with a safe flea powder, because flea's eggs drop off the body of the host and can lie dormant for months until conditions are right for them to hatch.

Given adequate care, a cat should live a long and healthy life. The average life-span has been increasing every year—it is now 17 years—but many have been known to live considerably longer.

The Psychology of Cats

The character of cats has long fascinated human beings. There seems to exist among cats an acceptance of a social hierarchy, a clear recognition that there are superior and inferior individuals. This can be clearly observed when several are together, when certain ones will defer to others at the food dish or favorite resting place.

The stocky Chartreux cat (above) comes from rural France. It has a very strong jaw softened by rounded cheeks.

These cream Persian kittens (left) and this short-haired baby cat show the irresistible appeal of all kittens, regardless of the degree of aristocracy in their ancestry.

A cat's dignity is a sacred thing. It does not like to endure any loss in this respect. Therefore, one cannot teach it to do any tricks that are not to its own advantage. The usual kinds of intelligence tests, such as the solving of mazes and recognition of color disks, give little insight into the cat's I.Q., since it generally will not respond to being tested. On the other hand, very difficult tasks can be learned by cats in order to obtain a desired objective.

As far as the cat's relationship with dogs is concerned, almost everyone is inclined to assume that they are natural enemies. It is true that dogs will often chase cats, just as they will chase after squirrels, yet cats and dogs, if they are given a chance to get acquainted with each other, are capable of living very happily together. A person who intends to keep both a cat and a dog should make sure that they are brought into the household together as kitten and pup. Even when grown to adulthood, they soon learn to accept one another as long as they are kept in separate rooms for the first few days and given an opportunity to get used to each other's strange scent gradually and thus to avoid a hostile first meeting.

When confronted with danger, a cat can be transformed into a snarling, hissing bundle of fury. Unlike the dog, which may run off, the cat will stand its ground, arching its back to appear larger. Most people think that the cat arches its back through fear, but naturalists have found that the real role played in feline psychology by this gesture is one of intimidation of the enemy.

The cat is naturally cautious and will not rush foolishly into situations without taking stock. Its response to sudden movement or noise is immediate.

Many household cats exhibit jealousy of either a new child or a new animal brought into the household. They react by refusing to eat or perhaps refusing to clean themselves.

For some reason, cats bring out very strong emotions in their human beholders. They are considered to be mean, vicious, ungrateful, and cowardly by some. To others, they are lithe, attractive, and esthetically satisfying. The truth is there are many aspects to a cat's personality, some of which are bound to find reflection in those who observe them. Cats have many postures, as shown at right and below, to indicate their emotional condition, and they use them regularly.

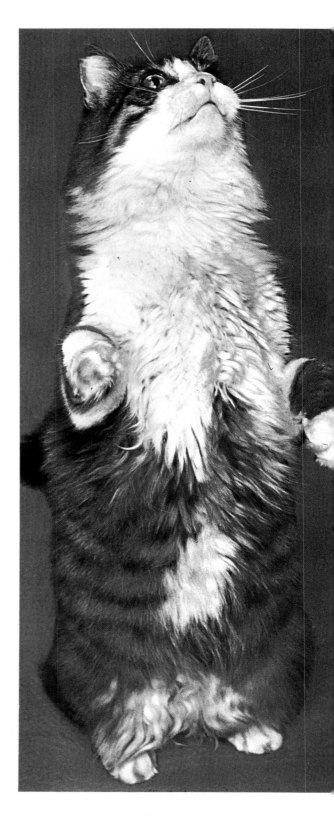

Some castrated males exhibit the same reactions that an intact male would in the presence of a female in heat. It has been observed that many pedigreed cats tend to show homosexual tendencies. A female might express aggressive behavior toward another female in heat. Studies have shown that female Siamese tend to be more neurotic than those of other breeds.

In the area of maternal disorders, cats have been known to kill their litters for apparently no reason. Also, many females experience false pregnancies. This only happens if a cat is unusually disturbed or nervous. The symptoms are an excessive appetite, a distended stomach and swollen, painful, discharging teats. Then the female will "adopt" and "mother" a soft item, such as a sock or a ball of wool or a small toy, and in some cases even take a young chicken or duckling, and treat it as its own.

It has been proven that cats also dream, but there is no way of telling whether these dreams are comparable to human dreams. Although the cat often purrs in its sleep, it seems very agitated at other times, and perhaps this indicates pleasant and unpleasant dreams. Since it is certain that cats have memories, dreams may be a reenacting of an experience that they have had during their waking hours.

A cat's first reaction to anything new is fear. In very short time, however, curiosity overcomes terror and a full investigation is undertaken. Note the unmistakable curiosity in the eyes of all the cats shown here.

The Mustelids— the Bloodthirsty Weasels

Modern members of the weasel family have evolved but little in some respects from their ancestral stock, the miacids who were also the ancestors of the civets, dogs and cats. The mustelids, which include not only the weasel proper but also skunks, badgers, otters, martens, minks and sables, among others, are to be found scattered all over the world with the exception of Australia, New Zealand and the Oceanic islands. Although one of their ancestors, which lived about 25 million years ago, was a weasel as big as a modern black bear, today's representatives range in size from the tiny weasel proper up to a 35-pound wolverine and the giant otter, which measures 6 feet including the tail. In spite of their modest size, they are unusually brave and generally highly aggressive animals with a decided taste for blood.

Like the miacids of 40 million years ago, the weasels as a family generally possess long lithe bodies and stocky legs. They come equipped with claws which are hooked, very sharp and nonretractile. Some are equipped with webbed feet and are at home in the water, others like to climb trees. They have specialized teeth for tearing tough meat. Their dental formula is not uniform but the most common formula is $I^{3/3}$, $C^{1/1}$, $Pm^{4/4}$, $M^{1/2}$, a total of 38 teeth. The canines are sharp and the carnassials well developed. Almost all have anal scent glands that secrete an unpleasant-smelling substance.

They usually dig their own dens, which may take the form of very long tunnels, but they also often take over other animals' holes. Gestation usually lasts from 12 to 16 weeks. They are unsocial creatures, living in couples; only rarely do they form small groups.

The family Mustelidae is divided into five groups or subfamilies: (1) the Mustelinae, or the weasels proper; (2) the Mellivorinae, or the honey badgers; (3) the Melinae, or the badgers; (4) the Mephitinae, or the skunks; and (5) the Lutrinae, or the otters.

As we have already mentioned, the 40-million-year-old miacids are the ancestors of all the weasels. Different genera had already assumed the forms of animals which we know today.

Plesictis, found in European rocks of the Oligocene epoch, was like a true mustelid. In North America, rocks of the Miocene period (25 to 20 million years ago) revealed fossil remains of an enormous mustelid the size of a jaguar but having an upper molar different from that of modern forms. The largest of all known mustelids, it was given the name *Megalictis*. It is often compared to a wolverine.

Fossil ancestors of the modern badgers have been discovered in European and Asiatic Miocene and Pliocene deposits. The skunks seem to be closely related to the badger. *Promephitis*, from Europe and Asia (Pliocene), is thought by many authorities to be a bridging form.

Certain members of the mustelids have a thick, dense fur highly esteemed by furriers. Indeed, the most hunted animals on the North American continent in the 18th century were the mustelids. Despite the fact that pound for pound they were the most able fighters on the North American continent, their very survival was threatened by trappers.

Mustelinae— the True Weasels

The mustelines, with their 11 genera and 32 species, constitute the most numerous subfamily among the mustelids. True weasels all have small heads, long snouts with long vibrissae ("whiskers") and rounded ears. They are extremely agile and arch their backs

(opposite page) Three striped skunks peer out of the rocky crevice in which they live.

(below) The cranium of a ferret shows teeth that are highly specialized for carnivorous function. The sharp canines and the well-differentiated carnassials are visible. The dental formula of the Mustelidae is not the same in the various genera. The ferret has 24 teeth.

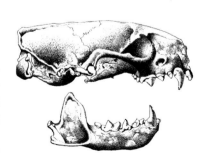

in normal movement. The fur of some species is of great commercial value.

The Ermine or Stoat (*Mustela erminea*) wears brown in summer and white in winter, a life-preserving coat, since the ermine lives in snowbound lands. It also has a black-pointed tail the year round. This distinguishes it from other species in this genus which have tails that change color with the seasons. This weasel whose winter coat is the symbol of royalty has a slender body and relatively long neck. The paws are hairy in winter but bare in summer, when the fur is light chestnut or reddish brown. The ermine is about 1 foot long, including the tail. The female is slightly smaller than the male.

It lives in both woods and open, stony terrain. It digs holes and tunnels and is an expert climber and swimmer. Naturally curious, it can be lured out into the open if you make a squeaking noise near its burrow. Mating takes place in the early summer, and there is a ten-month gestation period. The usual litter is from three to 13 young; at birth the young weigh less than one-tenth of an ounce. The young are born with a very fine mane of white hair on the neck and scattered hairs on the back. The brown-and-white fur pattern becomes evident at about two weeks. The eyes open at four weeks, and the young are weaned at five weeks.

Ermine attack prey larger than themselves, and when threatened they will attack man. They are especially valuable in destroying rats and mice around barns and granaries and also kill small birds, reptiles, insects, rabbits and earthworms. When hunting, the ermine emits a repetitive, trilling cry. It kills its prey with a lightning slash at the base of the skull; it does not suck blood. It often kills more than it can eat at one meal and only occasionally stores leftovers for future use.

This animal is found throughout Europe, Asia and America, particularly in the northern latitudes. In the Old World, it is called a stoat. In America, the ermine is called a short-tailed weasel.

The New World or Eastern Mink (*Mustela vison*) has a fur so valued in the coat mar-

ket that this animal has been the object of a murderous hunt which over the years has reduced its numbers considerably. Larger, stouter, more robust than the weasel, the mink is both an aquatic and land animal. It prefers to live in the shadow of pine trees which, however, it does not climb. Its fur is a beautiful chestnut brown with a white patch on the chin and traces of white or gray on the head and ears, as well as a dark

The ermine, like several other furry vertebrates, is characterized by the phenomenon known as seasonal "color dimorphism." In summer its coat is light chestnut in color, occasionally with reddish tints. In winter, the ermine is entirely white, except for the tip of the tail, which is black.

line running down about half the back. It hunts its food along streams and lake shores. It is chiefly nocturnal, feeding on small rodents, frogs, toads, swamp birds, hare, domestic fowls, fish and muskrats. It drags its kill off to its den, where it stores any surplus food for a future feast.

Adult minks measure about 2 feet in length including the tail; the females are somewhat smaller than the males. Mating occurs between February and April, and the gestation period lasts about six weeks. There are usually three or four young, who are born blind and remain that way for about one month. The young leave their mother after several months.

The native habitat of this mink includes Canada and the United States. Careful selection has led to animals with particularly fine furs, and today, there are mink farms

Although the weasel is the smallest of the carnivores, it is one of the most aggressive, as we see in this photograph of a weasel in combat with a snake.

in both countries where mink are bred and sold commercially.

The Black-footed Ferret (*Mustela nigripes*) was first discovered in 1851. It is now a very rare animal, and little is known about its habits. It is about 2 feet long and has unusual coloring—a red head with a black mask and a dark stripe down its back. Its undersides are yellow-buff, and the tail tip and legs are black. It is found in the Great Plains region, always associated with prairie dogs on which it preys. It has become almost extinct with the disappearance of its favored prey.

The European Weasel (*Mustela nivalis*) is the second-smallest carnivore, the smallest being the American **Least Weasel** (*Mustela rixosa*), which has quite similar habits.

The European weasel measures only about 8 inches when full grown, including the tail. It is an elegant and agile animal and a very aggressive fighter. The trunk, neck and head are slender. Its soft fur is cinnamon colored, with whitish underparts. The tail tip is usually darker than the rest of the body fur. It can be found inhabiting grassy or brushy areas and open woodland. It closely resembles the ermine, even having the same number of teeth, but the ermine is larger and has a proportionately longer tail. The weasel is not a good climber but is an excellent swimmer. It hunts all kinds of small vertebrates, including young hares and rabbits. When endangered, the weasel will attack man. It has been known to raid chicken coops and pigeon lofts, but it is also helpful to man, since it protects his crops by eating rodents. When taken young they make elegant and playful pets. The animal moves in small jumps, resting on its haunches. The weasel's cry, when alarmed, is a sharp *cree-cree!* The average litter is about five, which

A marbled polecat, which owes its name to the coloring of its fur, marked by brown and yellowish spots. Its tail is splendid, being very long and thickly furred.

are born in a den at any time of the year. Gestation usually lasts about six weeks, after which time the young are born with their eyes closed; they are nursed for about one month. They open their eyes at about 25 days, but they remain with their mother until almost full grown.

About ten species of weasels, all of the genus *Mustela,* range from Greenland throughout the Americas to Patagonia. In the Old World, they range from the Arctic throughout Europe and Asia. They are not found in India, Indochina or China.

The Old World or European Mink (*Mustela lutreola*) resembles the New World mink, although it is smaller. This animal also has a white throat, chin and upper lip. Today it is chiefly found in northern Europe. In the past it was more common in both central and western Europe. Mainly nocturnal, it breeds once a year in February or March.

The Siberian Mink (*Mustela sibirica*) is found in Russia from the Yenisey River eastward. It resembles a very large weasel, and its fur is dark brown, lightening to tawny and pale brown underneath the body.

The European Polecat (*Mustela putorius*), like so many others in the genus, uses a foul-smelling fluid to confuse its enemies, but since this animal is useful for keeping the house free of mice and rats, man has bred a domesticated polecat, the ferret, free of an offensive odor. It is also used for hunting rabbits, driving the rabbit from its burrow into the hunter's range. In its wild state, the polecat lives in dens or bushy regions, feeding on small vertebrates, including vipers, which it attacks without fear of being bitten. It measures about 2 feet long and has a broad muzzle, low rounded ears and small eyes. Mainly nocturnal and not very talkative, it makes murmuring sounds or small grunts.

Polecats mate in the spring and give birth to four or five young. They do not open their eyes for about a month but are able to live independent lives after about three months. This animal is found over most of Europe, as far south as the Mediterranean countries, including North Africa. When taken young, it can be domesticated; it will keep a house free of rodents.

The subspecies *Mustela putorius larvatus* is found in Tibet and Kashmir. The fur, long and rough, is often used for making brushes.

The Eurasian pine marten has a small head, a pointed snout, and round, protruding eyes. It lives almost entirely in the woods and is able to climb with great speed when chasing a bird, a squirrel or other small arboreal vertebrates. The female often gives birth to her young in birds' nests or in hollow trees.

The Old World sable (below), similar in appearance to the pine marten, supplies a pelt that is among the most expensive in the world. It is very soft with a suggestion of black on the back and feet, of gray on the snout and cheeks, and with a yellowish or reddish marking on the throat. Pelts differ slightly, one from another, but all have incomparable silky overtones, particularly in the darker parts.

The Marbled Polecat (*Vormela peregusna*), an Asiatic species, also has anal glands which secrete a foul-smelling fluid which it uses as a defense. When menaced, it screeches, grumbles and releases its secretion. Once found also in Europe, it now roams around the Caspian Sea and down to the southern part of Afghanistan. It is also found in central Europe, Rumania, Bulgaria, Russia, Israel and Iraq. It measures less than 2 feet and has a bushy tail. The back fur is spotted yellow and brown, the underparts are a shiny black. Its muzzle is brown, darkening to black, and it wears a white stripe on its forehead and at the nape of the neck. Preferring to prowl by night, it hunts the usual musteline diet of rodents, birds and reptiles. The female gives birth to three or four young in early spring.

The Pine Marten (*Martes martes*) is one of five members of this branch of the weasel family which can be found all over the world. The pine marten, a solitary elusive animal, lives in the forests of Eurasia, eastward to Siberia and southward to the Medi-

terranean. It differs from the stone marten, which also inhabits Europe, in the yellowish fur on its chest. Otherwise its handsome fur ranges from brown to black.

Adult males are usually about 2 feet long and weigh about 2 pounds. When it is relaxed, its voice is a soft murmur, but when excited, the murmur becomes a hiss and it mews and cries loudly. Its glandular secretion, used to confuse enemies, is very unpleasant, especially during the mating season. A very capable tree-climber, it is most active during summer nights, in contrast to the American marten, which prefers winter and snow. It also mates in summer. Gestation is about nine months, after which the mother gives birth to three to five babies. The young are born blind and remain so for about a month. They leave their mother at eight weeks of age. Young pine martens can be domesticated.

The Stone Marten (*Martes foina*) ranges from the Atlantic south of Scandinavia to the Urals in Russia and southward to Sikkim in the Himalaya Mountains. This animal differs

from the pine marten in the color of its throat and chest markings, being white instead of yellowish. The stone marten prefers the countryside to the forest. It climbs quite easily, and it has been known to hide out under woodpiles or in deserted buildings. When, as it often does, it invades henhouses and pigeon lofts, it massacres the fowl without quarter. It also eats fruits.

During the reproductive season, which may either be at the end of the winter or in the summer, the stone marten's cry is like that of an amorous cat. After a gestation period of eight or nine months, the female gives birth to four or five young, which are born blind and remain that way for about one month.

The pelt of the stone marten has less commercial value than that of the pine marten, but it is in demand. When hunting the stone marten, the hunter exploits the animal's ir-

ritability by making "annoying" noises at the entrance of the den; these cause the marten to come out into the open in a rage, thus exposing itself. When taken young, it can be domesticated.

The American Marten (*Martes americana*) is a handsome animal about 25 inches long, expert at streaking through tree tops in search of squirrels. It also travels easily over

(left) In spite of its aggressive temperament, the tayra, if captured when young, can be tamed. However, the slightest incident is enough to awaken its fierce instincts.

snow to hunt down mice and shrews. It also eats honey, berries and nuts. A dark black-brown, it has silver markings. It lives in the denser forests of Canada and the northeastern United States. Its chief enemies, aside from man, are the horned owl, the lynx and the fisher, another kind of marten.

The Sable (*Martes zibellina*) inhabits northern Europe and Asia. For centuries it has

been mercilessly hunted because of the commerical value of its coat. It measures about 2 feet long, about half of which is tail. The sable is fond of berries and honey. It leads a very active, primarily nocturnal life. In April the female bears four or five young after a two-month gestation period. The young are readily domesticated, and in captivity the sable is a fairly good-natured animal. In spite of this, domestic breeding for the sake of the pelt has not been successful.

The Yellow-throated Marten (*Martes flavigula* or *Charronia flavigula*) is more than 2 feet long, including an extremely long and bushy tail. The predominant color is a glossy brown-black, deepening to solid black toward the head, the nape of the neck, the saddle, the tail and the legs. The shoulders and the flanks are lighter in color, at times almost whitish. From the throat to the chest, the

(left) The pelt of the grison has a gray undercoat with either silky black or curly black-and-white overhair. The hair is longest on the backs, the flanks, and the tail.

dominant color is yellowish-brown, almost orange, and very bright. These animals have anal gland secretions, but the odor is not so strong as in the other martens. The yellow-throated marten is found in India, Burma, Indochina, Kashmir, Assam, Sumatra and southern China; it is lacking in Ceylon. It inhabits the high forest region where it can usually be found in groups of five or six. It hunts for food at night and during the day; its diet consists of small vertebrates, eggs and fruit.

The Fisher (*Martes pennanti*) looks like a large bulky cat. Despite its name, it rarely enters the water and eats fish only if it can steal another animal's catch. But it can whip a dog trained to fight bears and is one of the few animals which ventures to attack porcupines. It turns the rodent over and pounces on its underside, which is not protected by quills. A fisher may even chew off its own foot if caught in a trap. It was practically unknown until the mid-19th century, when its fur pelt began to be appreciated. It is about 3 feet long, including 12 inches of tail, and weighs about 10 pounds. Found in the northern United States and Canada, it lives around swamps and other bodies of water. The efforts of trappers and hunters have led

to its extinction in some areas. The fur is soft and silky, brown-black in color with gray areas on the head and neck. In some species, the fur lightens to a pale yellow. It reaches maturity at a year but does not normally breed until it is two years old. Mating occurs in April, and the mother carries its baby about ten months. After giving birth to two to four young, the mother can breed again within a week's time. The young remain blind about two months, but by three months they know how to hunt and are on their own at six months. Efforts have been made to domesticate it, but the fisher seems to prefer life in the wilderness.

The Tayra (*Tayra barbara*), a very savage member of the weasel family, matches the otter in size. Belonging exclusively to South and Central America, it can be found from southern Mexico to Argentina. Agile and an excellent climber, it prefers to live in hollow trees, clefts in rocks and the deserted burrows of other animals. In humid regions, its color is mainly black, but in dry regions its coloring is lighter and the throat markings yellow rather than red; in the dry savanna land, the color is tawny or creamy yellow and the chest and flanks white, a variety which provides us with a good example of protective coloration. Eggs play an important role in its diet, but it also feeds on other small mammals and birds and is particularly fond of honey. The females give birth to a pair of young in the spring.

The Grison (*Grison vittatus*) is also known as the **Hurone**. It is about 2 feet long, with a relatively short tail. Its coloration is very similar to that of a badger, light on top and dark underneath. It is found from southern Mexico to Peru and Brazil. The nostrils are placed to the side of the muzzle, and a white or yellow stripe runs along both sides of the head, extending down toward the neck. The pad of the foot is bare, and the foot itself is webbed. Grisons are sociable animals, usually seen in groups. They hunt small vertebrates, rats and birds. Its pelt is not in great demand because the fur and overhair are sparse. It lives for the most part in dens, crevices and tree hollows. In Argentina it is often domesticated and kept as a house pet, and the native hunters train them to track down chinchillas, which are valued for their pelts. The grison, like the tayra, eats eggs.

The Patagonian Weasel (*Lyncodon patagonicus*) is a small animal that is similar to the ferret in its habits but resembles the weasel in size and general appearance. Its coloring is distributed differently than in most wea-

The grison (left) is a mustelid native to Central and South America where it lives a congenial life with its fellows. It is a very sociable beast.

123

sels, being darker on the underparts and lighter above. The head has a yellow spot, from which two stripes of the same color run down to the flanks. A distinguishing feature is its dentition—it has only 28 teeth. It normally measures less than 2 feet long, half of which is tail. This weasel, with its rough pelt, is quite rare and limited to scattered open grassland localities in western Argentina and in Chile along the southern Argentine border.

The Zorille (*Ictonyx striatus*), also called the African, or striped, polecat, is found over a wide range of habitat. Its fur is thick and soft, glossy black in color, with stripes and spots of white. It has three white spots on the head, one between the eyes and the other two on each side of the head above the eyes. In some species, the three spots merge to form a frontal stripe. Four other white stripes, separated by three black stripes, run along the back and flanks from the white nape of the neck to the tail. The secretion

from its anal glands is so powerful that it can blind an enemy. The Sudanese call it "father of stinks" because the odor is so strong.

In general appearance the zorille very closely resembles the American spotted skunk, and they even have similar habits. The zorille and the skunk both carry their tails in the same way, and both emit the most unpleasant of odors when attacked. The zorille's body is long and stocky, the legs are short with hairy pads, the feet each have five digits and sharp claws, the head is broad, the muzzle is sharp, the eyes are small, the ears are short and rounded, and the fur is very thick. It has from 28 to 30 teeth. It measures from 1 to 1½ feet in body length, with the tail extending an additional foot. It is basically a nocturnal animal and is neither a good climber nor swimmer. The zorille inhabits Africa from Senegal, northern Nigeria, the Sudan, and Abyssinia to southern Africa. It is a slow-moving, fearless animal that

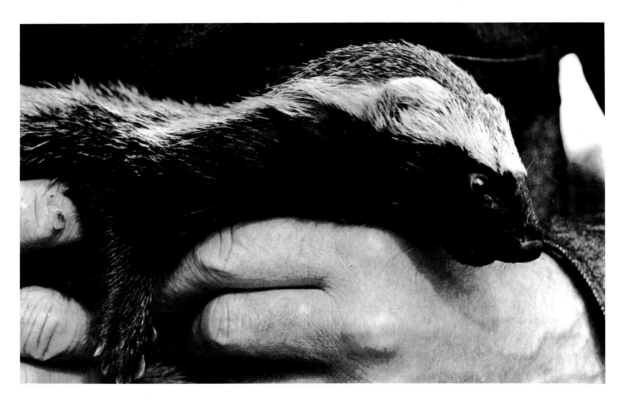

The grison used to be trained to ferret out chinchillas in much the same way that ferrets are used. This practice, however, is now illegal.

hides under thick brush or in the holes of other animals. It can be easily domesticated and does not use its protective odor unless it has been frightened. In many homes, the zorille is useful as a mouser.

The North African Banded Weasel (*Poecilictis lybica*) is very much like the zorille in appearance, except that it is smaller. As its name indicates, it inhabits North Africa, especially Libya, and is usually found in cultivated areas at the edge of deserts. Its tail is white and very bushy, but fortunately for the animal itself its fur, although of fair quality, is not greatly in demand, and thus it has been spared by hunters.

The African Striped Weasel (*Poecilogale albinucha*) is a small animal, about the size of a weasel. The upper head and neck are white, the back is black, and it has a white tail and two white stripes on its flanks. It is found in southern and central Africa and north to Congo.

African striped weasels are active both day and night. Frequently they travel in pairs or in family groups, spending much time on the ground but also climbing fairly well. They can emit a noxious secretion, which is strong and persistent but not quite so potent as that of the skunks. These weasels, although usually silent, can emit a loud shrieking sound when alarmed. The diet consists of small mammals and ground snakes and insects. Their method of killing snakes is much like that of the mongoose, consisting of repeated sallies that provoke the snake to strike over and over. When the reptile becomes tired, the striped weasel moves in, seizes the snake by the back of the head and kills it. They have been known to attack poultry, but their habit of ridding settlements of rats, mice and other vermin more than makes up for their depredations. Little is known of their reproductive habits except that the usual number of young is two. When taken as

The wolverine or glutton (left) has short legs, a broad head, and a rather squat, stocky body, all of which give it something of the appearance of a small bear. Although it inhabits cold, snowy areas like the weasel (below), it does not share the habit of color-changing during winter months.

The polecat on this page is about to enjoy a frog dinner, while the one on the facing page is investigating the possibilities of fungus growing on a tree.

juveniles, they can be easily tamed and make very rewarding pets.

The Wolverine (*Gulo gulo*) is the most ferocious of this ferocious group. It resembles a miniature bear armed with a skunklike smell for defense. Also called the glutton, it combines an enormous appetite with a strange kleptomania which can be a nuisance to the unwary trapper. It will creep into unoccupied tents and steal anything in sight, including rifles, axes, knives, dishes and even blankets, all of which it carries away and buries. Hunters in turn make use of the wolverine's skin for blankets and overcoats as well as trimming around the edges of parka hoods — that is to say, whenever the trapper can catch a wolverine, for such are its skills and guile

that it is almost impossible to trap. Few animals have waged so successful a war against man and his arts as has this wily lord of the weasels.

It has 28 very strong teeth and a talent for climbing trees, from which it is capable of jumping to attack a deer, lacerating its neck until it falls. The wolverine also feeds on small rodents and berries, but carrion is its preferred food. If desperate it will raid barnyards. Once these animals ranged throughout the northern two-thirds of Europe, North America and Asia but they have since been pushed northwards. Now they roam the forests of the Scandinavian peninsula, northern Russia, Poland and North America, especially Canada, where they live from ocean to ocean. Largest of the mustelines, it measures over 3 feet and weighs up to 40 pounds. The legs are short, giving it a stocky appearance. The fur is long, the head is broad, and the eyes are small and widely spaced. The wolverine's gait resembles that of a bear, for it walks on the soles of its forelimbs and only partially on the toes of the hindlimbs. Its back is slightly arched and its tail hangs down. The fur is thick, long, and glossy, being of a blackish-brown color on the back, tail, legs and stomach and a somewhat lighter ash-gray reddish on the shoulders and flanks. Breeding occurs between February and April. The litter ranges from two to five, usually being three, which nurse for eight to ten weeks. The young, born after a gestation period of eight weeks, have the adult color pattern in reverse and are driven from the maternal territory when they are about two years old.

Mellivorines — the Honey Badgers

The subfamily Mellivorinae includes only one genus with a single species in this subfamily.

The Honey Badger or Ratel (*Mellivora capensis*) is badgerlike in build, with rudimen-

a relatively stubby tail and stout legs. Its teeth are somewhat like those of the feline family. The female carries its young for six months, then gives birth to two babies. It eats rats, frogs, birds and insects and likes to live in dry woods where it can find termites. It can easily be tamed as a pet. It purrs when content and turns somersaults to attract attention, but when it is angered it cries out and will even bite its master. Above all, it stands its ground with a courage far greater than its size.

Mellinae — the True Badgers

There are only a few species in this subfamily, and they are all fitted with claws that make them prodigious diggers. Other than that, they have for the most part stocky bodies, long snouts and short tails. Their color tends to be darker on the underparts than on the back. The head is spotted black. Badgers are omnivorous, feeding on anything from larvae to carrion.

tary ears. It is one of the more courageous members of the weasel family, but it can also make an amusing pet. Found throughout Africa and from Arabia eastward to India, the ratel has a great fondness for honey, from which it derives its name. It will attack a hive without fear of being stung because its skin hangs loosely on its body. To find the source for its favorite food, the ratel uses the sparrow-sized honey guide, a small bird which flies before it and chatters loudly when it finds a hive. The ratel grunts to signal its presence, breaks open the hive, eats the honey and leaves the wax for the bird.

The ratel is generally black with long black hair on its paws, which have very strong claws permitting it to dig itself into the ground surprisingly fast in times of danger. It usually measures less than 3 feet, with

(left) The pine marten is generally solitary and is active day and night, summer and winter, in its search for carrion, insects and fruit, when in season.

The Old World Badger (*Meles meles*) is an expert burrower, capable of digging a highly complex labyrinth of underground tunnels and chambers where several generations of badgers can live together. Their homes are kept very clean. When they surface, these friendly, social animals play all kinds of games, including leapfrog. Physically this resident of Europe looks like a pig, especially in the shape of its snout. It has small eyes and ears and hairless feet. The fur on the back is a light yellowish-gray; two dark, almost black, stripes run from the snout to the top of the head, passing over the eyes and behind the ears. On the flanks, this badger has a more reddish coloration, and the underparts are a deep chestnut verging on black. The skin fits loosely, to the point that if the animal is held by the skin it can turn and bite. The fur is rough and thick, with long overhair that is used commercially for brushes. The anal scent glands secrete a very unpleasant odor.

Several geographical races are distributed throughout Eurasia except for northern Scandinavia, Sardinia and Asia north of the Himalayas. Old World badgers are nocturnal animals with shy, retiring habits; they sleep all day in large burrows. The badger has 38 teeth and feeds on small vertebrates as well as mushrooms, truffles, roots, fruit and honey. The period for mating is in the autumn, and after five or six months the female gives birth to from three to five young. The young are born blind and remain so for about ten days. In captivity, badgers can reach an age of 15 years.

The Hog Badger (*Arctonyx collaris*) has a woolly fur which is hard on top because of its rough overhair. It is basically a dirty-gray color, with dark, almost black, underparts. The head is elongated, having small eyes and tiny rounded ears. The snout is long, truncate, and mobile, similar to that of a pig. It is a nocturnal animal, hiding by day in crevices or dens. Its diet is mostly small animals, including earthworms, which are rooted out with the snout. In captivity the hog badger does not demonstrate much intelligent

(right) The polecat in its domesticated state is usually albino. It is used for ferreting out rats and rabbits and is referred to as a "ferret."

Weasels (left) are amazingly fast animals whose slender bodies allow them to enter any burrow or hole into which the head fits. They kill with speed and strength by biting at the base of the victim's skull.

(below) Wolverines are strong, solitary animals with a great sense of play.

behavior; instead, it is lazy and spends much of its time sleeping. When touched, it becomes angry, grunts and tries to bite. It habitually rears up on its hind legs. It inhabits most of China, northeastern India, Assam, Burma, Indochina, Thailand and Sumatra.

The Malayan Stink Badger (*Mydaus javanensis*) gets its name from the malodorous liquid that it can spray from its anal scent glands. Diluted, however, this secretion was used by ancient Javanese sultans to make their perfumes. When the stink badger uses the fluid as a defensive weapon it can spray it as far as 2 feet.

The badger's tail is very short, its eyes and ears are small. The fur is a dark chestnut that is lighter around the belly and chest and on a stripe on the back that runs from the

nape to the tail. It is about a foot and a half long. The fur is soft with a distinctly rough region on the head and neck, forming a small mane. The animal leads a nocturnal life and feeds on worms and other various small animals as well as vegetables. It is docile and easy to tame. The female gives birth to three or four young at a time. The stink badger is native to Java, Sumatra and Borneo, where it lives in mountainous forests. It is hunted by the natives for its meat.

The American Badger (*Taxidea taxus*) lives in the New World from southwestern Canada and the north-central part of the United States to central Mexico. These animals are fearless when cornered; they invariably stand their ground and fight. They have been reported as hunting in partnership with coyotes. Equipped with strong front legs and inch-long claws, the badger not only burrows its own living quarters but does not hesitate to invade those of others, such as gophers and prairie dogs. It travels by night from one burrow to the other, devouring the hapless occupants. Indeed, it will eat any animal it can catch. It also eats vegetation. While it can adapt to being in captivity, it does not make friends with humans. In comparison to the Old World badger, it has a broader head, but its habits are much the same. It measures about 3 feet in length, including a 6-inch tail. The snout is short and covered with hair to the nostrils. The fur on the back is a mixture of gray and yellowish-brown, while the underparts are gray or reddish. A long white stripe runs down the spine, and thin white stripes and spots mark the cheeks. Badgers breed in August and give birth to a litter of about five in late spring. Only in the coldest regions do they go into hibernation.

The Bornean Ferret Badger (*Melogale* or *Helictis orientalis*) was first classed as a member of the genus *Gulo*, the wolverines, which is a good indication of its outward appearance.

The body is long, measuring slightly under 2 feet, and the tail is an additional 12 inches. The shape of the head is elongated, the snout is long, flexible and hairless on top. A narrow band of bristles separates the flat rhinarium (the end of the snout, where the nostrils are) from the upper lip. Other characteristics include short, strong legs with hairless pads and compressed claws which are longer in the forefeet than in the hind feet. Its habits are similar to those of all the other badgers previously discussed. It inhabits Java and Borneo.

The ferret badger of Burma, Nepal and Indochina (*Melogale personata*) is a closely related species, except that it is slightly smaller and has a brownish-yellowish snout and a proportionately longer tail. A third similar species is the Chinese ferret badger (*Melogale moschata*) which is found in the forests of southern and central China, Assam and Formosa. This species has red-orange fur with a white stripe running over its head and

An American badger (opposite page) is photographed as he comes out of his burrow. A timid, rather awkward animal, the American badger stays in its burrow all day, coming out at night to catch small rodents, birds, or reptiles. A favorite prey is the prairie dog.

The honey badger, pictured below, adapts well to life in captivity. In the zoo, it attracts attention because of its habit of circling its cage, then stopping to turn a somersault in the same place each time.

An Old World badger (above) roots in the grass for the insects and mushrooms on which it feeds.

attacking animal, for skunks go through elaborate motions to display their conspicuous designs as though to remind the predator that he is attacking at his own risk. The subfamily is composed of three genera comprising ten species of skunks.

The Striped Skunk (*Mephitis mephitis*) raises its plumed 12-inch tail over its back when threatened and stamps its feet menacingly. Well aware of the power of its anal scent glands, these skunks rarely flee when confronted by animals much larger than themselves—including man. Their name is misleading, for these skunks vary considerably in their markings, some even being pure white or pure black. They measure 12 to 16 inches in length plus the tail. The head is small but long, the ears are short and round. The legs are fairly short. There are 34 teeth.

Its habits resemble those of its fellow species. The ability to spray the malodorous secretion on threatening enemies seems to vary with age. Skunks are primarily nocturnal and hunt mainly for insects, mice, birds' eggs, frogs and chickens. They vary their carnivorous diet with fruit. If not in hollow trees or crevices, they can be found in deep burrows, where the females give birth in the spring to litters ranging from six to ten young. The litter remains with the mother for about a year. Generally skunks do not hibernate, except in the coldest of climates. They are ingenuous and trusting animals, easily trapped by hunters attracted to their thick, soft fur. In spite of the unpleasantness associated with their scent glands, their meat has a very good flavor. The striped skunk can be found from Hudson Bay south into northern Mexico. Civilization does not seem to affect them adversely, as they are quite at home under buildings and are often found in towns and suburbs.

The Hooded Skunk (*Mephitis macroura*) is a species closely related to the striped skunk.

down its back; the underparts are dark. It feeds on small mammals and fruit. It is often kept around native huts as a destroyer of pest insects.

Mephitinae — Ten Kinds of Skunks

Aside from their well known defensive smell, the skunks have equally distinctive markings. These seem to serve as a warning to the

Its tail is the same length as its body, and black hairs pepper the white of the flank stripes. It is found from Arizona to Nicaragua. The hooded skunk has a white-backed color phase and a black-backed color phase.

The Spotted Skunks include two species, *Spilogale putorius* and *S. pygmaea*. The latter, not at all well known, is consistently smaller than the former. The spotted skunk is black with obvious white spots and short bands throughout the body and on the tip of the tail. It is smaller than the striped species and has a forehead blaze and beautiful silky fur. It is considerably more graceful in its movements than the striped species. Spotted skunks range from Puget Sound in the west to Maryland in the east and Panama in the south. *S. pygmaea* is known only on the Pacific coast of Mexico.

The Old World badger (left) like the American badger is a timid nocturnal animal. The difference between the Old World and the New World species lies chiefly in certain characteristics of the dentition. Badgers live in wild regions where they dig deep burrows. A large central den has various passages leading from it and surfacing at various points. The den is lined with moss and dry leaves.

The hog-nosed skunk has a magnificent tail which is almost as long as the rest of its body. A native of Latin America, it has a name in Spanish that means "little fox."

Their characteristic walk is with the tail straight up or bent over the back until the tip touches the head, with the long hairs hanging down like a shawl. When confronted by an enemy, the spotted skunk rears up on its hind legs, ready to discharge its secretion.

The spotted skunk is a nocturnal creature, preferring places where it is easy to hide. Usually in the spring, but in southern areas at any time of the year, the female gives birth to about six young who remain with their mother for about one year.

In the perfume industry, the anal secretion of the spotted skunk is used in very small amounts as a fixative for certain fragrances. The feeding habits of the spotted skunks are similar to those of striped skunks. In the summer they eat vegetable matter, in winter

they eat rodents, other small mammals and occasionally carrion. Spotted skunks usually den underground, but they are good climbers and occasionally take shelter in trees. As many as eight individuals have been found spending the day in dens lined with dry vegetation. These animals are very playful with one another when they are in groups. They are quite aggressive in their defensive tech-

Magellan. *Conepatus* is the only genus of skunk in South America. They range from 12 to 20 inches in body length, with a tail from 6 to 16 inches long. They have low, stocky bodies, pointed heads and hairless muzzles that resemble pig snouts. The eyes and ears are small, the fur is long, thick and black, sometimes with reddish tints. They prefer open terrain where vegetation is sparse. They

The striped skunk can be found in southern Canada and throughout the United States. It is a small animal, about the size of a cat and is slow moving and deliberate. It comes out only at night, spending the day at rest in its den.

niques, actually standing on their forefeet and backing into the aggressor if the latter does not retreat immediately.

The Hog-nosed Skunks of the genus *Conepatus* comprise about six species varying in size and pattern. They are distributed from the southwestern United States to the Strait of

burrow near the base of trees and stay in dens all day. Their nocturnal habits are similar to those of the striped and spotted skunks. Some South American hog-nosed skunks are immune to the venom of rattlesnakes. Rattlers exposed to skunk musk show a reaction of alarm, suggesting that skunks must frequently attack these poisonous snakes.

135

Lutrinae—Otters Around the World

Otters are mammals that catch fish, and every feature of their bodies is designed to improve their adaptation to aquatic life. They have broad, flat heads; long, slim, streamlined bodies and webbed feet. Their teeth are perfectly shaped for seizing and holding fish. Playful and intelligent, they can be easily trained. Their fur, short, dark-brown and lustrous, is prized by commercial furriers.

River Otters of the genus *Lutra* catch fish in the water but eat them on dry land. Capable of remaining underwater for long periods of time, they can also function quite well on land. If frightened, however, they show which habitat they prefer, for they run to hide in the water. They are not exclusively fish-eaters, feeding also on birds, frogs, crayfish and water rats. They do not seem to be affected by frigidly cold water, and they can be seen floating peaceably in the freezing water, their paws crossed over their bellies.

River otters dig their own dens on the river banks and only rarely move into the abandoned quarters of another animal. As a rule they are solitary animals, but occasionally several individuals join in a group. Very playful, they love to slide down snowy hummocks on river banks and to play tunneling games. River otters are found in a wide variety of inland streams, in estuaries and sea coves, in all continents except Australia.

While the number of species is great, the differences between them are small. Some twelve distinct species are recognized. River otters are dark brown in color on the underparts. The skin around the lips and on the chin and throat is red-gray. They have elongated cylindrical bodies and flattened heads with a broad snout, small eyes, small ears, thick lips and very long whiskers. The front legs are short and the hind legs and feet large, with all of the toes webbed. The pads of the feet are partly covered with hair, and on land the otter can place its feet almost flat on the ground. It can also close its nostrils and ears when swimming underwater. The glands, which secrete a musky odor, are located near the genital openings in both males and females. When fully grown, males measure about 5 feet, including the muscular rudder-like tail, which is about 2 feet.

The Common European Otter (*Lutra lutra*) is also known as the Old World otter. With its waterproof coat and sinuous body, it is perfectly adapted to aquatic life. Easily tamed, it can be taught to enter and leave the water on command. This otter is native to Europe, Asia and North Africa. It reaches maturity between two and three years of age and mates early in the spring of the third year. The mother carries its young about nine weeks, then gives birth to them in a den that has been well lined with grasses and moss. The young are about the size of mice at birth and are born blind, but by the time they are nine months old they are able to take care of themselves. Subspecies live in the same areas

The giant otter (lower left) is a South American species that is relentlessly hunted for its beautiful pelt. Its fur is very short, soft, and of a pale brown, almost ivory, color. The giant otter is much larger than others of the otter group.

To a river otter (below), water is its favorite environment, wherever it may find it. When on land, it moves with curious snakelike contortions and manages to cover a lot of ground.

Although the otter's movements on land are clumsy, it is a great swimmer and a fantastic diver. It can remain underwater for long periods of time because of its great lung capacity. It usually hunts from the bank, from which it can spot its prey and dive to the capture with great accuracy.

as *Lutra lutra*, and another allied species, *Lutra lutra nair*, is native to southern India and Ceylon. It is smaller and grayer in color than the common European otter. The Indian otter can be found living in the vast lagoons or even in the sea, close to shore. They are easy to tame and follow their masters like dogs. They can be trained to catch fish and bring them to the fisherman or to drive fish into a net. Another subspecies is the **Golden**

like teeth. In the Amazon basin the species *Lutra plantensis* and *L. incarum* can be found. Still another South American species is *L. provocax*.

A characteristic distinguishing the **American Otter** (*Lutra canadensis*) from its Old World counterpart is the extension of the bare skin above the nose to beyond the nostrils. This species has a blue-black back, with lighter

Otter (*Lutra lutra aureobrunnea*) from the Nepalese mountains.

In South America, there is a distinct species, *Lutra felina*, a smaller otter than *L. lutra*, with no claws, a short snout and cat-

shading on the chin, throat, chest and stomach. Its habits are basically the same as its European cousin's. The American otter plays the game of sliding on smooth slopes made slippery by mud or snow. Its preferred diet is fish and crustaceans. In April the female gives birth to two or three young, which it then cares for until autumn. It is hunted for its fur and is usually trapped at its sliding ground. It is found in North America as far north as the glacial seas and is particularly abundant along the banks of the Mackenzie River and in the Adirondack Mountain streams. Its numbers are diminishing. River otters have lived as long as 20 years.

areas around the mouth, throat and the sides of the neck. The tail is about 2 feet long, very flat and covered with thick woolly fur. The neck and head are particularly large. The smooth-coated otter can be found in considerable numbers on the Malay Peninsula of Burma, in Assam and in central India. A species which is closely related to the smooth-coated otter is the Malay, or Sumatra, otter (*Lutra sumatrana*), which has a hairy snout.

The Canadian otter, like all otters, prefers an aquatic life.

The Smooth-coated Otter (*Lutra perspicillata*) is an Asian species, about the same size as the European, or common, otter. Its coloration is reddish-brown, with lighter shades appearing on its underparts. It has whitish

The Giant Otter (*Pteronura brasiliensis*) is well named. Its body is 4 feet long and its tail another 3 feet. This flat efficient swimming organ, with its edges projected on either side, has inspired the alternative name of flat-tailed otter for this species. Aside from its size, it differs from other otters in that it prefers day to night. Another peculiarity is the high-pitched shriek it utters, at the same time raising the forepart of its body out of the water.

Giant otters make their dens in burrows or under tree roots along the river. Like river otters, it moves to dry land before eating the fish caught in the water. It also feeds on eggs and birds. Its head is quite large and flat on top. The body is cylindrical, the legs short, the feet webbed. Its snout is very hairy, bare only along the rims of the nostrils. The coloring is uniformly light brown and slightly lighter on the upper head and neck. There is a large white-to-cream patch on its chest.

This animal has always been hunted because of the commercial value of its hide, which is used in the furrier trade. The giant otter, however, has an excellent defense which makes it very difficult to catch—it dives deep under the water the moment it is threatened.

The Oriental Small-clawed Otter (*Amblonyx cinerea*) has as its outstanding characteristic strongly reduced claws, which are almost absent in the adult. This species measures about 2 feet in length, with the tail adding another 18 inches. The upper parts are dark brown, the underparts are brownish-gray. A few whitish spots are visible on the lips, throat and the sides of the neck. Its habits are basically the same as those of the other otters, and it is also tamed by fishermen to be used as a helper. It inhabits southern Asia, Borneo, Java, Sumatra and the Philippines. It seems to favor high mountain altitudes. Mussels, snails and crabs are favored items in its diet.

The African Clawless Otter (*Aonyx capensis*) is larger than the European or common otter. Body and tail together may be as long as 5 feet. The toes are quite elongated, especially in the forepaws, but there are no claws. Curiously, the feet seem to be without webbing except for a narrow webbing at the base

of the toes on the hind feet. The fur is rich, soft and woolly with silky overhair. Its color is chestnut, shading to reddish on the sides and underparts. There are white markings on the cheeks, throat and chest. The cheek teeth are large and very strong, perfect for

The Cape or Clawless otter is widely distributed in Africa. It is similar to the Oriental small-clawed otter.

cracking mollusk shells. The fur is considered to be of little commercial value. These otters are basically solitary and are rarely found even in pairs or small groups. They are mainly nocturnal animals, and when not in search of food they spend their days in dens near the water.

Naturalists think that the clawless otter does not dig its own den. It is known to spend some time on land and occasionally to raid henhouses. This animal inhabits all of Africa south of the Sahara. The habitat ranges from open coastal plains and semiarid country to dense forests, but the otters are always found near a permanent body of water. They prefer the giant pools and sluggish streams, in contrast to African *Lutra* species, which occur in parts of the same range. Unlike *Lutra*, which is mainly a fisheater, they feed almost exclusively on crabs and other crustaceans. This species also eats turtles, fish, frogs, lizards, aquatic birds and small mammals. It never eats off the ground, but picks its food up with its front paws. After a gestation period of about 63 days, two to five young are born, usually in the spring. Young clawless otters remain with their mother for about one year. If acquired when young, they make intelligent and charming pets.

The African Small-clawed Otter (genus *Paraonyx*) has three species, all from Congo and West Africa. The animals are all about 3 feet long and uniformly dark in color. The toes of the forefeet are only partially webbed, those of the hind feet are fully webbed. The claws are small and blunt. These animals are believed to feed mainly on soft matter, such as eggs and frogs, rather than fish.

The Sea Otter (*Enhydris lutris*), until recently, was threatened with extinction. It had become so rare that its fur fetched a very high price. Spurred on by the value of the highly prized fur, hunters chased sea otters

A river otter (left) shows its streamlined swimming shape. This species has large claws as well as extensive webbing on its feet.

for over 170 years; by 1910 they were almost extinct. Now, protected by an international treaty, they are on the increase. Rather different from the other otters, it is particularly well adapted for its sea life. The hind feet, very broad and fully webbed, function as oars. The molars and premolars have flat, broad, round crowns that provide grinding surfaces on which to crack the hard shells of shellfish. The sea otter also has the curious habit of floating on its back on the surface of the water with its lunch laid out on its stomach. It places a flat stone on its chest which it uses to crack open mollusks by pounding the shells against the stone. This makes it one of the few animals to qualify as a user of tools. It is however, equally content to eat on dry land.

It inhabits the sea beds along the coast, even sleeping there, moored to a cluster of seaweed. It once inhabited the entire Pacific Ocean coast of North America from lower California to the Aleutians and the Bering

Sea. Colonies of them can be found off the coast of central California, western Alaska and parts of the Bering Sea. The valuable fur is essentially dark brown, tinted gray in the young and silvery in the adults. Unlike other marine mammals, sea otters do not have an insulating layer of fat beneath the skin. For protection against cold water, they depend entirely on the layer of air trapped between the long fibers of hair. If the fur is soiled, the insulating quality is lost. Male otters measure up to 5 feet in length, including the 12-inch tail. The body resembles that of a seal, with short front limbs and a small tail. Its feet are short and square, and both feet and tail are hairy. It is the only carnivore with four incisor teeth in its lower jaw. It feeds on sea urchins, abalone, mussels, clams and large snails. Extremely playful, these otters make amusing although very independent pets; their insatiable curiosity leads them to examine everything in the household.

The sea otter (right) has a small rounded head, very small eyes, and hairy ears. Its hairless, wrinkled nostrils and its thick lips give it a curious appearance. Its dark-brown pelt is highly prized by furriers.

Index *Italicized page numbers refer to illustrations.*